Frayed Union:

How Enemies Within are Destroying America

Jonathan Koch

Published by: Jonathan koch

Table of Contents

Introduction

America, a country of remarkable resilience and innovation, stands as a testament to human ambition and the enduring quest for democracy and freedom. From its early days as a fledgling nation, America has drawn strength from its diverse population, bountiful resources, and pioneering spirit. These strengths have propelled it to the forefront of global leadership in various fields, including technology, economy, and culture. Yet, beneath this remarkable facade lies a foundation that has been tested time and again by internal and external forces seeking to exploit its vulnerabilities.

At the heart of America's story is a paradox: the very elements that make it strong also expose it to unique risks. The open society that fosters creativity and progress also makes it susceptible to ideological subversion. The freedoms Americans cherish can be manipulated to create division and dissent. As we embark on this exploration of America's fragile foundation, it is crucial to understand the historical context that has shaped both its strengths and vulnerabilities.

Throughout history, America's greatest adversaries have often come not from distant lands but from within its own borders. This concept of enemies within is not new; it has roots that stretch back to the nation's earliest days. Espionage, ideological subversion, and systemic weaknesses have all played their part in testing the nation's resolve. These internal threats are insidious because they operate under the radar, quietly eroding the very fabric of society while appearing, at least on the surface, to be harmless or even beneficial.

Espionage, a practice as old as civilization itself, has always had a profound impact on national security. In America's case, foreign powers have long sought to infiltrate its institutions, steal its secrets, and undermine its stability. The Cold War era saw espionage reach unprecedented levels, with spies embedded in government agencies, scientific laboratories, and even cultural institutions. These agents worked tirelessly to gather information, sow discord, and weaken the nation's defenses from the inside out.

Ideological subversion, another potent tool in the arsenal of America's enemies, capitalizes on the nation's commitment to free expression and open debate. By introducing and promoting radical ideologies, these adversaries aim to fracture societal cohesion and turn Americans against one another. This strategy thrives in an environment where freedom of thought and speech are protected, making it challenging to identify and counteract subversive activities without infringing on cherished civil liberties.

Systemic weaknesses, inherent in any complex society, further complicate the landscape. America's vast and intricate systems

—be they political, economic, or social—are prone to exploitation. Corruption, inefficiency, and bureaucracy create fertile ground for those who seek to weaken the nation from within. These weaknesses can manifest in various forms, such as electoral meddling, financial manipulation, or the spread of misinformation. Left unchecked, they corrode trust in institutions and fuel a sense of cynicism and disillusionment.

As we delve deeper into the intricacies of America's fragile foundation, it becomes clear that understanding these internal threats is essential to preserving the nation's integrity. In the chapters that follow, we will explore specific instances of espionage, ideological subversion, and exploitation of systemic weaknesses. We will examine how these threats have evolved over time, adapting to new technologies and changing societal norms. By shedding light on these hidden dangers, we hope to foster greater awareness and resilience among readers.

In today's interconnected world, the challenges facing America are more complex than ever before. The digital age has introduced new avenues for espionage, with cyber-attacks and data breaches becoming increasingly common. Social media platforms serve as battlegrounds for ideological subversion, allowing disinformation to spread rapidly and widely. Systemic weaknesses are magnified in a globalized economy, where financial crises or supply chain disruptions can have far-reaching consequences. Navigating this intricate web of threats requires vigilance, adaptability, and a deep understanding of the principles that underpin American society.

While the focus of this book is on identifying and understanding internal threats, it is equally important to recognize the strengths that have enabled America to withstand these challenges thus far. The nation's robust legal framework, vibrant civil society, and resilient democratic institutions provide a solid foundation upon which to build. By leveraging these strengths and addressing vulnerabilities head-on, America can continue to thrive in the face of adversity.

It is our hope that this exploration will inspire readers to take an active role in safeguarding the nation's future. Whether through civic engagement, education, or simply staying informed, each individual has a part to play in fortifying the fragile foundation of America. In doing so, we honor the legacy of those who came before us and ensure that the values of democracy, freedom, and justice endure for generations to come.

In conclusion, America's story is one of both triumph and tribulation. Its historical strengths have propelled it to great heights, while its vulnerabilities have provided fertile ground for internal threats. By examining the concepts of espionage, ideological subversion, and systemic weaknesses, we gain insight into the delicate balance that defines this great nation. As we move forward, let us do so with a renewed sense of purpose and determination, committed to preserving the ideals that make America a beacon of hope and possibility.

Frayed Union: How Enemies Within are Destroying America

Chapter 1

The Seeds of Division

The seeds of division are deeply embedded within the fabric of society, manifesting through various forms of polarization and conflict. These divisions often begin subtly but grow into significant rifts that impact communities on multiple levels. As societal polarization intensifies, it leads to the fragmentation of collective identities and the erosion of social bonds. Differences in opinions become more extreme, and the willingness to engage with differing viewpoints diminishes. This process is not just a superficial separation but one that deeply affects the core of communal life, altering how individuals interact with each other and view their place within society.

In this chapter, we delve into the origins and influences that foster societal divisions, exploring the multifaceted nature of these divides. We will examine how identity politics and cultural clashes contribute to heightened tensions and the ways in which these issues manifest in daily life. Additionally, we will discuss the role of external and internal actors in deepening these divisions, including the spread of misinformation and disinformation. The chapter will also touch upon the media's influence in shaping public perception and the interplay between various forces that exacerbate societal rifts. Through this exploration, we aim to provide a comprehensive understanding of the factors that drive societal polarization and the potential pathways toward mitigating these divides.

Exploration of Societal Fault Lines

Polarization plays a critical role in creating divides within communities. It is the process through which opinions on issues become more extreme, leading to increased opposition and decreased willingness to engage with differing viewpoints. Social polarization often begins subtly, but as it intensifies, it can create deep rifts within communities, fragmenting collective identities and eroding social bonds.

Identity politics is a significant mechanism for group differentiation and conflict. This concept involves political positions based on the interests of specific social groups. While identity politics can empower marginalized groups by giving voice to their unique challenges, it also tends to prioritize group identities over shared commonalities. This emphasis on distinct group identities often escalates tensions between different segments of society, fostering resentment and mistrust. For example, political movements centered around race, gender, or sexual orientation may strengthen intra-group solidarity, but simultaneously, they can exacerbate inter-group divisions as different groups compete for recognition and resources.

Cultural clashes arising from conflicting values, beliefs, and traditions further deepen societal divides. These clashes can manifest in various ways, from disagreements over social norms and practices to outright hostility towards cultural expressions perceived as alien or threatening. Cultural differences often originate from deeply ingrained historical experiences and societal structures. For instance, debates over immigration policies frequently highlight cultural differences, where native populations may feel their values are being undermined by the influx of new customs and traditions. Such clashes not only strain interpersonal relationships but can lead to broader social exclusion and discrimination.

These fault lines considerably impact social cohesion and unity. As societal polarization intensifies, trust between community members deteriorates, making collaborative efforts and mutual understanding increasingly challenging. Social cohesion relies heavily on shared values and collective goals. When communities become polarized, these foundational elements are weakened, resulting in fragmented societies where cooperation becomes rare and conflict more commonplace. The erosion of social cohesion leads to an environment where individuals are more likely to view those outside their immediate group with suspicion, further perpetuating cycles of division.

Moreover, the consequences of such polarization extend beyond interpersonal relations to affect institutional trust and democratic functionality. Institutions that once acted as mediators of social conflicts and promoters of public good can become battlegrounds for polarized groups. Political parties, educational institutions, and even religious organizations might be co-opted to advance specific group agendas, undermining their neutrality and effectiveness. This shift not only obstructs governance but also delegitimizes these institutions in the eyes of large segments of the population, further deepening societal fissures.

Addressing these underlying issues requires a multifaceted approach that promotes dialogue and understanding across diverse groups. Initiatives aimed at fostering inclusive communities and promoting cross-cultural exchanges can play a pivotal role in mitigating tensions. For example, community-based programs that encourage joint problem-solving activities among people from different backgrounds can help build bridges of understanding. Creating platforms for open dialogue where individuals can share their perspectives without fear of judgment fosters a sense of empathy and respect.

Education systems also have a vital role to play in countering societal polarization. Incorporating multicultural education and diversity training in school curricula can help young individuals appreciate the value of different perspectives. Schools that emphasize critical thinking, empathy, and cultural competence prepare students to navigate a diverse world more effectively. These educational initiatives should be complemented by media literacy programs that empower individuals to critically assess information sources and combat misinformation, which frequently exacerbates polarization.

Policy interventions should address structural inequalities that contribute to social divisions. Policies promoting economic equality, social justice, and inclusive governance can reduce disparities and provide marginalized groups with greater opportunities for participation. Economic policies that bridge the gap between affluent and impoverished communities can alleviate feelings of marginalization and discontent. Similarly, reforms aimed at reducing political polarization, such as campaign finance reform and redistricting reform, can restore trust in democratic institutions by ensuring fair representation and encouraging bipartisan collaboration.

Influence of Foreign and Domestic Actors

Understanding the role of various actors in deepening societal divisions requires a multifaceted approach, examining both external and internal influences that contribute to these rifts. In an increasingly interconnected world, foreign actors play a significant part in exacerbating internal conflicts within societies. These actors, often state or non-state entities, deploy a variety of tactics designed to sow discord and weaken national unity.

One of the primary methods used by foreign actors is the spread of misinformation, disinformation, and malinformation. Misinformation refers to false information not intended to cause harm, whereas disinformation is deliberately misleading and maliciously crafted to manipulate public perception. On the other hand, malinformation involves facts presented out of context to mislead or harm. These tactics aim to create confusion, erode trust in democratic institutions, and deepen social divides. A notable example is the interference by foreign powers in election processes through online campaigns disseminating falsehoods about candidates or policies. By undermining the electoral system's integrity, these malign actors succeed in creating a polarized electorate suspicious of the legitimacy of the democratic process (Foreign Influence Operations and Disinformation | Cybersecurity and Infrastructure Security Agency CISA, n.d.).

In addition to foreign interference, domestic political entities and interest groups also play a crucial role in amplifying societal divisions. Political parties often exploit existing social fault lines to consolidate their voter base, employing rhetoric that accentuates differences rather than commonalities. Interest groups, whether representing economic, racial, or ideological interests, may adopt similar strategies, pushing for policies that benefit specific groups at the expense of broader social cohesion. For instance, lobbying efforts by influential organizations can skew public policy and further entrench social divisions. The competitive nature of politics encourages a focus on divisive issues, leading to a fragmented society where consensus becomes increasingly elusive.

The media's role in shaping public perception and fueling discord cannot be overstated. Traditional media outlets, driven by the need for viewership and revenue, often resort to sensationalism and polarization. News coverage that emphasizes conflict and controversy attracts more attention, inevitably fostering a divided audience. The rise of social media has compounded this issue, as algorithms prioritize content that evokes strong emotional reactions, regardless of its veracity. This echo chamber effect reinforces pre-existing biases and drives wedges between different societal groups based on varying interpretations of the same events. Propaganda, whether state-sponsored or otherwise, further manipulates public opinion by presenting skewed narratives that align with specific agendas. The interplay between media sensationalism and propaganda creates a fertile ground for societal division, making it challenging for individuals to discern objective truth amidst a barrage of conflicting information.

Historical instances provide valuable insights into how both external and internal forces manipulate societal fault lines for specific outcomes. During the Cold War, both the United States and the Soviet Union engaged in psychological warfare, spreading propaganda to influence public opinion in different countries. These efforts were aimed at weakening adversaries by exploiting social tensions, thereby achieving strategic geopolitical advantages. Domestically, the civil rights movement in the United States saw various interest groups and political entities either supporting or opposing the push for equality, highlighting how internal actors can shape societal trajectories through advocacy and opposition.

More recently, the Brexit referendum in the United Kingdom showcased the confluence of foreign influence, domestic political maneuvering, and media impact. Foreign actors reportedly used targeted social media campaigns to sway public opinion, while domestic political entities capitalized on nationalist sentiments. Media coverage amplified these messages, creating an environment where misinformation thrived, ultimately influencing the referendum's outcome. This case underscores the intricate dynamics between different actors and their collective ability to open societal rifts for political gains.

Insights and Implications

The exploration of societal fault lines highlights the multifaceted origins and influences that foster divisions within communities. From polarization and identity politics to cultural clashes, these elements intertwine to create a complex landscape of conflict and fragmentation. The intensifying divisions erode social cohesion, making collaboration and mutual understanding challenging. As trust diminishes, institutional credibility suffers, further exacerbating societal rifts. Addressing these issues requires comprehensive strategies that promote dialogue, inclusiveness, and critical thinking.

Efforts to mitigate these divisions must encompass educational reforms, policy interventions, and community-based initiatives. Education systems should emphasize multicultural learning and media literacy to equip individuals with the skills necessary to navigate diverse viewpoints critically. Policies aimed at reducing economic inequalities and promoting inclusive governance can alleviate feelings of marginalization. Community programs fostering cross-cultural exchanges can bridge gaps and build empathy among different groups. By implementing such measures, societies can strengthen social bonds and restore a sense of unity amidst diversity.

Chapter 2

Economic Subterfuge

Economic subterfuge, a term encompassing various forms of financial manipulation and exploitation, poses severe threats to the global economy. Adversaries exploit these vulnerabilities through sophisticated cyber attacks, economic espionage, and illicit financial flows. This multifaceted issue exposes weaknesses in critical sectors such as finance and trade, enabling hostile entities to destabilize economies and gain illicit benefits. By delving into the intricacies of such economic exploitation, it becomes evident that adversaries meticulously tailor their tactics to exploit specific vulnerabilities, posing significant risks to economic stability and security.

In this chapter, we will explore the numerous ways adversaries exploit economic vulnerabilities to their advantage. We will delve into the methods employed in cyber attacks and economic espionage, illustrating how these tactics disrupt financial systems, steal sensitive information, and destabilize markets. Additionally, we will examine the role of illicit financial flows, including money laundering and terrorist financing, in undermining economic stability. Through detailed examples and analysis, we aim to shed light on the regulatory gaps that facilitate these activities and the need for stronger international cooperation to mitigate these risks.

Examination of Economic Vulnerabilities Exploited by Adversaries

Economic vulnerabilities provide lucrative opportunities for adversaries to exploit for their benefit. Identifying the key sectors susceptible to such exploitation is crucial in understanding and addressing these threats. The finance and trade sectors, due to their central role in the global economy, are particularly vulnerable. Financial institutions manage vast amounts of capital, and any breach in their systems can lead to significant economic disruptions. Adversaries often target these institutions to steal funds, manipulate markets, or disrupt financial services. Similarly, the trade sector, which involves the movement of goods and services across borders, is prone to exploitation through tactics like under-invoicing, over-invoicing, and trade-based money laundering.

Adversaries employ various tactics to exploit these vulnerabilities, each tailored to the specific weaknesses they identify. One common tactic is the use of cyber attacks. Through sophisticated hacking techniques, adversaries can infiltrate financial systems, access sensitive data, and even manipulate transactions. These cyber attacks can have devastating effects, causing financial losses, eroding consumer confidence, and destabilizing markets. Another tactic is economic espionage, where adversaries steal trade secrets, proprietary information, and intellectual property to gain a competitive edge. This not only undermines the targeted companies but also weakens the overall economic stability of nations. Illicit financial flows, including money laundering and terrorist financing, are another major threat. By channeling illicit funds through legitimate financial systems, adversaries can support criminal activities and further destabilize economies.

Regulatory gaps play a significant role in enabling economic subterfuge. In many cases, outdated or lax regulations fail to keep pace with the evolving tactics of adversaries, leaving critical sectors exposed. For example, insufficient cybersecurity frameworks in financial institutions can create easy entry points for cyber attacks. Additionally, gaps in international trade regulations may allow adversaries to exploit discrepancies between different countries' laws. These regulatory weaknesses make it easier for adversaries to conduct illegal activities with minimal risk of detection or prosecution. Strengthening regulatory frameworks and enhancing international cooperation are essential steps in closing these gaps and reducing the risk of economic subterfuge.

Globalization has significantly increased the interconnectedness of economies, creating new opportunities and challenges. While globalization has facilitated economic growth and development, it has also increased vulnerabilities. The interdependence of global financial markets means that a disruption in one part of the world can have far-reaching consequences. For instance, a cyber attack on a major financial institution in one country can trigger a chain reaction, affecting markets worldwide. Similarly, the global nature of trade makes it easier for adversaries to exploit cross-border regulatory disparities. As supply chains span multiple countries, the risk of counterfeit goods, industrial sabotage, and other forms of economic subterfuge increases. Addressing these vulnerabilities requires a coordinated global effort, with countries working together to enhance security measures and harmonize regulations.

Impact of Cyber Attacks

Understanding the consequences of cyber attacks on economies is crucial for both policymakers and businesses. Cyber attacks, particularly sophisticated ones like ransomware, have far-reaching impacts that go beyond immediate financial losses. Ransomware attacks involve malicious software that locks data or systems until a ransom is paid. These attacks are increasingly common and can significantly disrupt economic activities.

The economic impact of ransomware and other cyber attacks can be assessed through multiple lenses. First, there's the direct cost of paying ransoms. For instance, in 2021, the Colonial Pipeline Company paid nearly $4.4 million to regain access to their systems after a debilitating ransomware attack. However, these costs often pale in comparison to the financial burden of recovery and mitigation efforts. Companies spend significant amounts on cybersecurity experts, system restorations, and security upgrades to prevent future breaches. According to Natalucci et al., 2024, the financial sector alone accounts for a substantial portion of cyber incidents due to the sensitive nature of the data involved.

Recovering from cyber attacks also incurs indirect costs which can be even more damaging. These include reputational damage, loss of consumer trust, and decline in stock prices. The infamous data breach at Equifax in 2017 serves as an example where the company incurred over $1 billion in penalties, and the long-term impact on consumer confidence was profound. Consumers become wary of engaging with organizations perceived as vulnerable to cyber threats, leading to decreased transactions and weakened market positions.

Further compounding these issues is the effect on consumer confidence and market stability. A major cyber attack can undermine trust in financial institutions and markets, causing panic and abrupt movements in financial assets. Such instances can lead to market selloffs or, in extreme cases, runs on banks as consumers and investors rush to secure their funds. The Central Bank of Lesotho experienced such disruptions when a cyber attack halted their national payment system, preventing domestic bank transactions and causing widespread economic disturbance (Natalucci et al., 2024).

This erosion of consumer confidence not only affects the attacked entity but also has ripple effects across the economy. For example, smaller banks in the US have faced modest but persistent deposit outflows following cyber incidents, demonstrating how interconnected the financial ecosystem is (Natalucci et al., 2024). When consumer confidence dips, it can lead to reduced spending, lower levels of investment, and consequently, slower economic growth.

Preventive measures and robust cybersecurity protocols are essential to mitigate these risks. While individual firms bear responsibility for securing their networks, there is a strong argument for public intervention. Firms might lack the necessary incentives to fully address cyber risks, particularly those with potential systemic impacts. Public policies and governance frameworks must evolve to keep pace with the growing digital landscape and geopolitical tensions that elevate cyber threats (Natalucci et al., 2024).

One effective preventive measure involves developing a comprehensive cybersecurity strategy at the national level. Such strategies should be supported by dedicated regulations and supervisory capacities that regularly assess the cybersecurity landscape. This includes identifying potential systemic risks from interconnectedness and concentrations, especially from third-party service providers. Encouraging "cyber maturity" among financial firms, where board-level engagement with cybersecurity expertise is standard, could help bolster defenses against attacks.

Adopting frameworks like the National Institute of Standards and Technology (NIST) can also guide organizations in improving their cybersecurity posture (Brando et al., 2022). The NIST framework outlines five core functions—Identify, Protect, Detect, Respond, and Recover—that help institutions establish a robust defense mechanism. Identifying critical resources and associated risks allows firms to focus their protective measures effectively. Implementing advanced detection systems ensures timely identification of intrusions, while thorough response and recovery plans minimize downtime and financial losses.

In addition to these frameworks, regular training and awareness programs for employees play a vital role in fortifying cybersecurity. Human errors remain one of the leading causes of successful cyber attacks. By educating staff about phishing scams, proper password management, and safe online practices, companies can significantly reduce their vulnerability.

Furthermore, collaboration between private and public sectors is pivotal. Sharing threat intelligence and best practices can enhance collective resilience. Governments may consider incentivizing information sharing by providing legal protections or financial support for companies that participate in shared cybersecurity initiatives.

Lastly, investing in advanced technologies like artificial intelligence and machine learning can provide a competitive edge in detecting and mitigating cyber threats. These technologies offer real-time monitoring and predictive capabilities that can anticipate and counteract attacks before they cause significant harm. However, this reliance on advanced tech also necessitates rigorous oversight to manage new vulnerabilities that could emerge from these systems being targeted themselves.

Economic Espionage and Illicit Financial Flows

Economic subterfuge is a complex and multifaceted issue involving the manipulation of economic systems through various illicit activities. Central to this are economic espionage and illicit financial flows (IFFs), both of which play significant roles in undermining economic stability and global security.

Defining Economic Espionage and Examples

Economic espionage involves the illegal acquisition of trade secrets or proprietary information from businesses, often to benefit foreign entities. This can be achieved through various means, including cyber attacks, physical theft, or the infiltration of corporations. For example, one of the most notorious cases is the 2010 incident where Chinese hackers infiltrated Google's servers, stealing intellectual property and accessing the email accounts of human rights activists. Another instance occurred when an employee of a major automobile manufacturer was caught attempting to steal blueprints for a new car model on behalf of a competitor.

Economic espionage not only threatens individual companies but also has broader implications for national security and economic competitiveness. By siphoning off critical technological advancements or sensitive business strategies, adversaries can gain an unfair advantage in global markets, leading to substantial financial losses and reduced innovation.

Methods Used for Illicit Financial Flows, Including Money Laundering

Illicit financial flows refer to the movement of funds across borders in violation of national or international laws. These flows often conceal illegal activities such as tax evasion, corruption, and money laundering. Money laundering, one of the primary methods used in IFFs, involves the process of making illegally-gained proceeds appear legal by disguising their origins.

Methods of money laundering include:

1. **Placement**: Introducing illegal funds into the financial system, often through banks or casinos.
2. **Layering**: Conducting a series of complex transactions to obscure the origin of the funds. This may involve transferring money between multiple accounts, using shell companies, or investing in high-value items like real estate or art.
3. **Integration**: Re-entering the laundered money into the legitimate economy, making it difficult to trace its illegal origins.

For instance, a common scheme involves over-invoicing or under-invoicing in international trade. Companies might inflate the value of goods they are exporting to another country, allowing them to transfer excess funds abroad under the guise of legitimate business transactions.

International Implications and Challenges in Tracking IFFs

The international implications of IFFs are profound, affecting both developed and developing countries. Developing nations, in particular, suffer greatly as illicit outflows strip away resources that could be used for development projects, public services, and infrastructure improvements. As noted in a study by Herkenrath (2014), these illicit financial flows often exceed the amount of official development assistance received by developing countries, severely hampering their economic growth and social development.

Tracking and combating IFFs present several challenges:

1. **Jurisdictional Issues**: The transnational nature of illicit flows makes it difficult for any single country to track and regulate them. Different legal frameworks and levels of enforcement across countries complicate cooperation and coordination efforts.
2. **Complex Financial Networks**: The sophisticated methods used in money laundering, such as layering through multiple jurisdictions and using anonymous shell companies, make it challenging to trace the origins and destinations of illicit funds.
3. **Limited Resources**: Many developing countries lack the resources and technical expertise needed to effectively monitor and curb illicit flows. This limitation allows criminal organizations to exploit regulatory gaps and weak enforcement mechanisms.

Proposing Solutions to Mitigate Risks

Mitigating the risks posed by economic espionage and illicit financial flows requires a multi-faceted approach involving both national and international measures.

1. **Strengthening Legal Frameworks**: Establishing robust legal frameworks to criminalize economic espionage and tighten regulations on financial transactions can deter illegal activities. Countries should adopt comprehensive anti-money laundering (AML)

laws in line with international standards, ensuring consistency and cooperation across borders.

2. **Enhancing International Cooperation**: Greater collaboration among countries is essential to combat IFFs effectively. This includes sharing intelligence, harmonizing legal standards, and assisting in investigations and prosecutions. Initiatives such as the Financial Action Task Force (FATF) play a crucial role in setting guidelines and fostering international cooperation.

3. **Building Capacity**: Providing technical assistance and capacity-building support to developing countries can enhance their ability to detect and prevent IFFs. This may involve training law enforcement officials, improving financial monitoring systems, and modernizing regulatory frameworks.

4. **Public-Private Partnerships**: Collaboration between governments and the private sector, particularly financial institutions, can improve the detection and reporting of suspicious activities. Banks and other financial entities should adopt stringent AML measures, including customer due diligence (CDD) and transaction monitoring protocols.

5. **Leveraging Technology**: Utilizing advanced technologies such as artificial intelligence (AI) and big data analytics can aid in identifying patterns and anomalies indicative of illicit activities. These tools can

enhance the efficiency and effectiveness of monitoring and enforcement actions.

6. **Promoting Transparency**: Increasing transparency in financial transactions and corporate ownership structures can reduce opportunities for illicit activities. Implementing public registries of beneficial ownership and requiring disclosure of financial interests can help authorities and the public scrutinize and hold accountable those engaging in suspicious activities.

Case Studies of Industries Targeted

Economic subterfuge presents a clear and present danger to many industries, with adversaries exploiting economic vulnerabilities through various means. This section aims to provide real-world examples of how different industries are targeted by such nefarious activities.

One glaring example of economic subterfuge is seen in the tech industry, where data breaches and intellectual property theft are rampant. A notable case study involves the massive cyber attack on Sony Pictures Entertainment in 2014. The attackers, allegedly linked to North Korea, managed to steal a tremendous amount of data including unreleased films, confidential emails, and personal information of employees. Such breaches not only incur immediate financial losses due to data theft and system restoration but also have long-term repercussions including loss of consumer trust and damage to brand reputation. Another high-profile incident includes the series of attacks on

U.S. defense contractors aimed at stealing valuable military technologies. The Center for Strategic and International Studies (CSIS) recorded numerous instances where Chinese actors were involved in stealing American military innovations like the F-35 fighter jet and missile systems. These thefts have placed national security at risk while delivering strategic advantages to foreign adversaries.

The manufacturing sector is another significant target of economic subterfuge. Counterfeit goods and industrial sabotage are two major issues plaguing this industry. One poignant example is the counterfeit electronics market, which costs companies billions of dollars each year. These fake products often mimic successful brands and are sold at reduced prices, thereby undercutting legitimate businesses and tarnishing their reputations. In addition, industrial sabotage has wreaked havoc on manufacturing plants across the globe. In 2010, for instance, the Stuxnet worm targeted Iran's nuclear facilities, causing substantial damage to its centrifuges. This sophisticated malware attack highlighted the vulnerability of industrial control systems and underscored the potential for adversaries to cripple critical infrastructure through covert operations. The impact of such activities on supply chains and production capabilities cannot be overstated, leading to significant economic ramifications.

The energy industry has also been a prime target for cyber attacks, particularly those affecting critical infrastructure. In 2015, Ukraine experienced one of the most well-documented cyber attacks on a power grid, resulting in widespread power outages affecting hundreds of thousands of residents. The attack, attributed to Russian hackers, demonstrated the susceptibility of energy infrastructure to cyber threats. Similarly, the 2021 Colonial Pipeline ransomware attack in the United States disrupted fuel supplies along the East Coast, causing panic buying and fuel shortages. These incidents reveal the catastrophic potential of cyber attacks on energy grids, highlighting the need for robust cybersecurity measures to protect these vital assets.

The broader economic implications of targeting these vital industries are profound. When adversaries successfully infiltrate and compromise key sectors like technology, manufacturing, and energy, the ripple effects can be far-reaching. For instance, intellectual property theft in the tech industry may discourage innovation and investment, leading to slower technological advancements and diminished global competitiveness. The proliferation of counterfeit goods undermines legitimate businesses, reduces tax revenues, and poses significant health and safety risks to consumers. Industrial sabotage can disrupt supply chains, elevate production costs, and erode consumer confidence in the reliability of products.

Cyber attacks on energy infrastructure can have devastating consequences for national economies, impacting everything from transportation to healthcare. When power grids are targeted, the resultant blackouts can halt production lines, paralyze communication networks, and impede essential services. The economic cost of such disruptions can run into billions of dollars, as seen in cases like the Colonial Pipeline attack. Moreover, the threat of future attacks could compel governments and organizations to divert substantial resources towards bolstering cybersecurity defenses, further straining economic resources.

In this chapter, we explored how adversaries exploit economic vulnerabilities through various means such as cyber attacks, economic espionage, and illicit financial flows. The discussion highlighted the finance and trade sectors as particularly susceptible due to their central role in the global economy. Cyber attacks can infiltrate financial systems, leading to significant disruptions and loss of consumer confidence. Economic espionage undermines companies by stealing trade secrets, while illicit financial flows support criminal activities and destabilize economies. Regulatory gaps and the interconnected nature of global markets further exacerbate these threats, making it imperative to enhance security measures and international cooperation.

Addressing these vulnerabilities requires a multifaceted approach involving strengthened regulatory frameworks, improved cybersecurity protocols, and enhanced international collaboration. National strategies and public-private partnerships are critical in mitigating the risks posed by these economic threats. Advanced technologies like artificial intelligence can help detect and counteract attacks, but they also require rigorous oversight. By combining efforts at both national and international levels and leveraging modern tools and techniques, we can better protect our economic systems from adversaries seeking to exploit their weaknesses.

Chapter 3

Ideological Subversion

Ideological subversion examines how beliefs and values can infiltrate and reshape societal institutions. This chapter delves into the mechanisms through which ideological subversion manifests within key areas of American society, focusing on its subtle yet profound impact. The exploration begins with academia, where curriculum alterations and the influence of professors play a significant role in propagating specific ideologies. By shaping educational content and classroom discussions, these academic changes can affect students' perceptions and critical thinking abilities profoundly. Similar infiltration patterns extend to media and cultural institutions, each wielding substantial power over public opinion and societal norms.

This chapter provides an in-depth analysis of how ideological subversion operates in education, focusing on curriculum adjustments and the role of academic thought leaders. It also examines the interplay between media ownership, framing, and social media algorithms in spreading particular viewpoints. Additionally, the chapter explores the role of cultural institutions like arts, literature, and religious organizations in promoting specific ideologies, thereby influencing societal values. Through detailed examples and case studies, readers will gain a comprehensive understanding of the multifaceted nature of ideological subversion and its potential consequences for American values and democratic processes.

Ideological Infiltration in Academia

Ideology plays a significant role in shaping educational systems, particularly through curriculum changes designed to reflect certain ideologies. The curriculum is a powerful tool for imparting knowledge and values, thus it is often manipulated to promote specific ideologies. For instance, when the dominant ideology within a society emphasizes nationalism, the curriculum may prioritize national history, culture, and achievements while marginalizing or omitting other perspectives. This selective presentation of information can serve to reinforce the status quo, ensuring that students internalize the values that support existing power structures.

One critical aspect of how ideology infiltrates education is through the influence of academic thought leaders and professors. These individuals shape the intellectual environment of educational institutions and significantly impact the development and delivery of the curriculum. Professors often bring their own ideological beliefs into the classroom, consciously or unconsciously affecting the material they choose to teach and their interpretation of that material. When academic thought leaders advocate for certain ideologies, they can create a ripple effect throughout the educational system, influencing textbooks, teaching methodologies, and even educational policies.

Moreover, the promotion of specific political or social viewpoints in classrooms is another way through which ideology affects education. Teachers, acting as intermediaries between the curriculum and students, have considerable discretion in how they present information and encourage discussion. This latitude allows educators to subtly or overtly infuse their teachings with particular ideological perspectives. For example, a teacher might emphasize the importance of civic engagement and social justice, encouraging students to think critically about societal issues and take action. Alternatively, a teacher might focus on traditional values and the preservation of societal norms, shaping students' perceptions in a different direction. This variance in teaching approaches illustrates how classrooms become arenas for ideological battles, where diverse viewpoints contend for influence over young minds.

The impact of this ideological infusion on student perception and critical thinking abilities cannot be overstated. Ideological subversion in education has the potential to mold not only what students learn but also how they learn to approach information and ideas. A curriculum heavily laden with a singular ideological perspective can limit students' exposure to alternative viewpoints, stifling their ability to engage in critical thinking and independent analysis. In an educational environment where one ideology dominates, students may struggle to develop the skills necessary to question assumptions, analyze evidence, and form reasoned conclusions based on diverse sources of information.

Conversely, an educational system that encourages exposure to multiple perspectives and fosters critical discussion can enhance students' critical thinking abilities. By engaging with a variety of viewpoints, students learn to navigate complex issues, weigh contradictory evidence, and appreciate the nuanced nature of most real-world problems. This kind of education equips students with the analytical tools needed to become informed, reflective, and active citizens capable of contributing thoughtfully to democratic processes.

To understand the practical implications of these concepts, it is useful to examine specific examples. Consider a high school history class that focuses predominantly on the achievements and contributions of the dominant cultural group within a country. Such a curriculum might omit or downplay the experiences and perspectives of marginalized groups, creating a skewed understanding of history among students. In contrast, a more inclusive curriculum that incorporates diverse voices and experiences can provide a richer, more accurate depiction of history, fostering empathy and a deeper understanding of social dynamics.

Similarly, the presence of influential academic thought leaders who champion various ideologies can be observed in higher education. Universities known for their progressive ethos might feature prominent scholars advocating for social change and reform, while more conservative institutions might host academics emphasizing tradition and continuity. These ideological leanings shape the intellectual climate of each institution, influencing both faculty and students.

Classroom practices further illustrate the impact of ideology on education. A teacher promoting a particular political viewpoint might use current events to highlight issues aligned with that viewpoint, encouraging students to see the world through a specific ideological lens. Alternatively, a teacher committed to fostering critical thinking might present multiple perspectives on controversial issues, guiding students to explore these perspectives and arrive at their own informed conclusions.

The long-term effects of ideological influence on education are profound. Students educated within a system that prioritizes critical inquiry and diverse viewpoints are likely to develop strong analytical skills and an appreciation for complexity. They become more adept at navigating a world characterized by competing ideologies and conflicting information. On the other hand, students whose education is dominated by a single ideological perspective may find themselves less equipped to engage meaningfully with differing viewpoints, potentially leading to polarized thinking and reduced capacity for constructive dialogue.

Understanding the ideological dimensions of education also highlights the importance of educational advocacy. Stakeholders—students, parents, educators, and community members—can work together to promote an inclusive and balanced curriculum that reflects a wide range of perspectives. Advocacy efforts can include participating in school board meetings, supporting policies that foster diversity in educational content, and encouraging professional development for teachers focused on critical pedagogy.

Media as a Tool for Ideological Subversion

In understanding how media propagates certain ideologies, it is essential to first explore the control of media ownership by ideological groups. Media conglomerates often have substantial influence over the content they disseminate, shaping public perception and opinion. These conglomerates might be driven by specific political, economic, or social agendas that align with their interests. For example, certain media companies may lean towards conservative or liberal perspectives, which can significantly impact the type of news and information presented to the audience. This ownership control allows these ideological groups to prioritize stories that fit their narrative while downplaying or ignoring those that do not.

The concept of framing and bias in news reporting further exacerbates this issue. Framing refers to how news stories are presented to the audience, including what information is highlighted and what is omitted. This selective presentation can lead to a biased portrayal of events, subtly influencing the audience's understanding and interpretation. For instance, the coverage of a political protest might focus on the violent activities of a few participants rather than the peaceful demonstrations of the majority. Such framing can create a skewed perception, aligning with the objectives of the controlling ideological group.

Entertainment media also plays a crucial role in subtly influencing public opinion. Unlike direct news reporting, entertainment media, such as movies, TV shows, and music, embeds ideological messages in more approachable formats. For example, a popular television series might portray certain social issues or lifestyles in a favorable light, indirectly encouraging viewers to adopt similar views. Over time, repeated exposure to these messages can shape individuals' beliefs and values, aligning them with the intended ideology.

Moreover, social media algorithms contribute significantly to the propagation of ideologies by promoting echo chambers. Echo chambers refer to environments where individuals are exposed primarily to information and opinions that reinforce their existing beliefs. Social media platforms use sophisticated algorithms to tailor content based on users' past interactions, leading to a personalized feed that reflects their preferences and biases. Consequently, users are less likely to encounter differing viewpoints, resulting in a polarized and fragmented society. This phenomenon not only amplifies ideological divides but also hinders constructive dialogue and understanding between opposing perspectives.

Media ownership and control by ideological groups play a pivotal role in shaping the narratives presented to the public. By determining which stories are covered and how they are reported, these groups can effectively guide public discourse in a direction that aligns with their interests. The concentration of media ownership in the hands of a few powerful entities raises concerns about the diversity of perspectives available to the audience. When a limited number of voices dominate the media landscape, it becomes challenging for alternative viewpoints to gain traction.

Framing and bias in news reporting further solidify the influence of ideological groups. News organizations, consciously or unconsciously, employ framing techniques that emphasize certain aspects of a story while downplaying others. This selective emphasis can alter the audience's perception of events, steering them towards a particular interpretation. For example, a news outlet with a liberal bias might frame a government policy negatively, highlighting its potential drawbacks while neglecting its benefits. Conversely, a conservative-leaning outlet could focus on the policy's positive aspects, creating a more favorable impression. Such framing strategies align with the ideological orientation of the media owners, reinforcing their agenda through subtle manipulation.

Entertainment media serves as another powerful tool for ideological influence. Unlike news reporting, which is often scrutinized for bias, entertainment media operates with a level of creative freedom that allows for the integration of ideological messages in less obvious ways. Through compelling storytelling, relatable characters, and engaging plotlines, entertainment media can convey ideological themes that resonate with audiences on an emotional level. A television show, for instance, might depict progressive social changes as desirable and inevitable, subtly encouraging viewers to embrace similar viewpoints. Over time, these repeated portrayals can shape societal norms and values, reflecting the ideology embedded within the content.

The role of social media algorithms in promoting echo chambers cannot be overstated. These algorithms are designed to maximize user engagement by curating content that aligns with users' preferences and beliefs. While this personalization enhances user experience, it also creates insular environments where individuals are exposed primarily to like-minded perspectives. As a result, users become increasingly insulated from opposing viewpoints, reinforcing their existing beliefs and reducing the likelihood of encountering dissenting opinions. This phenomenon exacerbates ideological polarization, as individuals are less likely to engage with diverse perspectives and more prone to dismissing contrary viewpoints.

Cultural Institutions and Ideological Promotion

In the landscape of ideological subversion, cultural institutions play a pivotal role in shaping societal values and propagating specific ideologies. These institutions, ranging from arts and literature to religious organizations and public events, serve as conduits for disseminating ideas that can significantly influence the cultural and political fabric of society.

Arts and literature have always been influential in molding societal values. Through novels, paintings, films, and other forms of artistic expression, creators convey powerful messages that can reflect, critique, or reinforce prevailing ideologies. For example, during the Harlem Renaissance, African American writers and artists used their work to challenge racial stereotypes and advocate for social change, thus fostering a sense of pride and solidarity within the black community. Similarly, dystopian novels like George Orwell's "1984" have highlighted the dangers of totalitarianism, thereby shaping public consciousness about the importance of freedom and democracy.

Religious organizations also play a crucial role in the propagation of ideologies. Religion is often intertwined with cultural identity and can be leveraged to promote specific worldviews. Religious leaders can influence their followers through sermons, teachings, and community activities. For instance, the Social Gospel movement in the early 20th century used Christian ethics to address social justice issues, advocating for labor rights and economic equality. Conversely, some extremist groups have exploited religious doctrines to justify acts of terror and propagate radical ideologies, showcasing how religion can be used to further both positive and negative agendas.

Public events and festivals provide a platform for pushing certain narratives and ideologies to a broader audience. These events are not merely celebratory but often carry underlying messages that can shape public opinion and reinforce societal norms. Political rallies, national holidays, and cultural festivals can all serve as stages for ideological dissemination. For example, Independence Day celebrations in the United States reinforce patriotic sentiments and national unity, while events like Gay Pride parades promote acceptance and equality for the LGBTQ+ community. Such gatherings create a sense of community and shared purpose, making them effective tools for spreading specific ideologies.

Cultural institutions do not operate in isolation; they frequently interact with political movements, either supporting or challenging the status quo. This interaction can be seen in how governments use cultural policies to promote nationalistic ideologies or how opposition groups utilize cultural expressions to resist authoritarian regimes. The UNESCO program on cultural policy, mentioned in Alasuutari and Kangas (2020), highlights how international bodies can influence national cultural sectors, encouraging countries to develop policies that preserve cultural diversity while promoting shared global values.

Furthermore, the connection between cultural institutions and political movements can amplify the impact of ideological subversion. During the Civil Rights Movement in the United States, music, literature, and religious congregations played an integral role in mobilizing support and spreading the message of equality and justice. Songs like "We Shall Overcome" became anthems of resistance, while churches provided safe spaces for organizing and strategizing. This synergy between cultural expressions and political activism demonstrates the potent force of cultural institutions in driving societal change.

The influence of cultural institutions on societal values and ideologies is profound and multifaceted. Arts and literature offer a mirror to society's soul, reflecting its triumphs and tribulations while challenging individuals to think critically about their beliefs and actions. Religious organizations provide moral frameworks that guide behavior and decision-making, often reinforcing or contesting prevailing ideologies. Public events and festivals bring people together, creating opportunities for communal reflection and ideological dissemination. Finally, the interplay between cultural institutions and political movements underscores the dynamic nature of ideological subversion, highlighting the power of culture in shaping the political landscape.

Propaganda, Misinformation, and Foreign Influence

In examining methods of spreading propaganda and misinformation, including foreign involvement, it becomes evident that these tactics have evolved significantly and continue to impact American society profoundly. The ability to discern between truth and fabricated information is increasingly crucial as these deceptive practices grow more sophisticated.

Tactics used in propaganda campaigns are multifaceted and often rely on psychological manipulation. One common tactic is the use of emotional appeals to create a strong response from the audience. By tapping into emotions such as fear, anger, or patriotism, propagandists can sway public perception more effectively than through logical arguments alone. Additionally, repetition of key messages reinforces the intended narrative and makes it more likely for individuals to accept the information as true over time.

Another tactic involves cherry-picking facts or presenting half-truths. This selective presentation of information allows propagandists to construct a misleading but seemingly credible story. By omitting crucial details or context, they can distort reality and guide the audience to specific conclusions. Propagandists also frequently employ simplification, reducing complex issues into binary choices, making it easier for people to take sides without understanding the nuances involved.

Examples of misinformation in mainstream media highlight how even reputable sources can become conduits for false narratives. Misinformation can spread rapidly when picked up by major news outlets and social media platforms. For instance, during election cycles, false reports about candidates or policies can gain traction quickly, influencing voter opinions and behavior. High-profile cases like the Pizzagate conspiracy during the 2016 U.S. presidential election illustrate the severe consequences of such misinformation, which led to real-world violence based on completely unfounded claims.

Case studies of foreign influence operations targeting American society reveal the strategic nature of these efforts. Russia's disinformation campaign is a prominent example. State-funded media outlets like RT and Sputnik disseminate Russian narratives globally, amplifying content that aligns with their geopolitical goals. According to the State Department's Global Engagement Center, these organizations often work in concert with other pillars of Russia's disinformation ecosystem, enhancing the credibility and reach of their messaging (Disarming Disinformation, 2024).

Foreign actors also exploit social media to amplify their influence, creating fake accounts and automated bots to steer conversations and propagate divisive content. During the 2016 U.S. presidential election, Russian operatives utilized Facebook and Twitter to spread misleading stories and sow discord among voters. A Buzzfeed analysis found that the most widely shared fake news stories generated millions of interactions, outpacing legitimate news from established sources (West, 2017). These tactics demonstrate how foreign entities can manipulate the digital landscape to undermine democratic processes and societal cohesion.

The analysis of the effects on public trust and national security underscores the broader implications of propaganda and misinformation. Trust in media has significantly declined, with a large portion of the population doubting the accuracy of news reports (West, 2017). This erosion of trust makes it easier for false narratives to take root and harder for the public to distinguish fact from fiction.

The impact on national security is also profound. Disinformation campaigns can destabilize societies by polarizing communities, eroding faith in democratic institutions, and even provoking violence. The confusion and doubt sown by these campaigns create an environment where citizens are less likely to support government initiatives and more prone to questioning official policies. In extreme cases, this can lead to resistance against necessary measures for public safety, further exacerbating societal fractures.

Guidelines to counteract propaganda and misinformation focus on several key areas. Enhancing news literacy is essential, particularly in educational settings where young people can learn to critically evaluate information sources. Governments and institutions should fund programs that teach individuals how to recognize credible news and identify biased or false information. Encouraging a diverse media diet is another critical step. Consuming news from various reputable sources can provide a more balanced perspective and reduce the likelihood of falling victim to echo chambers or confirmation bias.

Additionally, fostering transparency in media production can help rebuild public trust. News organizations must prioritize ethical journalism, disclose potential conflicts of interest, and correct errors promptly. Supporting investigative journalism is also crucial; thorough reporting can expose and counteract disinformation efforts, shedding light on the sources and strategies behind them.

Combating the financial incentives for fake news can mitigate the spread of misinformation. Social media platforms and advertising networks play a significant role here. By demonetizing content that spreads false information and promoting content from reputable sources, these platforms can discourage the creation and dissemination of misleading material.

Finally, strengthening cooperation between governments, tech companies, and civil society is vital. Coordinated efforts can more effectively detect and respond to disinformation campaigns, leveraging technology to track and neutralize harmful content while respecting free speech and privacy rights.

The chapter delved into the ways ideological subversion seeps into key societal institutions and its profound impact on American values. By exploring the manipulation of educational curricula, it highlighted how specific ideologies can dominate the classroom, shaping not only the knowledge imparted to students but also their critical thinking skills. The role of academic thought leaders and teachers in perpetuating these ideologies through subtle or overt means was also discussed, illustrating the far-reaching influence on young minds. Furthermore, the chapter examined how a balanced and inclusive curriculum could foster critical discussion and enhance students' ability to engage with diverse perspectives.

In addition to education, the chapter examined the media's role as a vehicle for ideological subversion. Media ownership by ideological groups and the use of framing and bias in reporting were shown to shape public perception significantly. Entertainment media and social media algorithms further contribute by embedding ideological messages and creating echo chambers that reinforce existing beliefs. The chapter concluded by emphasizing the interplay between cultural institutions and political movements, highlighting arts, literature, religious organizations, and public events as conduits for disseminating ideas that mold societal values. Understanding these dynamics is crucial for recognizing the profound impact of ideological subversion on American society.

Chapter 4

Political Manipulation

Political manipulation represents a profound challenge to democratic processes, involving various tactics employed to influence political opinions and outcomes. These strategies are executed by an array of actors, including governments, political parties, extremist groups, and private entities, each utilizing their unique resources and methods. Understanding the complexities of these operations is essential to fully grasp their impact on governance and public trust.

This chapter delves into different techniques used in political manipulation, such as disinformation, propaganda, astroturfing, and false amplification. It elaborates on the agents behind these manipulations, ranging from foreign governments to domestic political campaigns and extremist groups. The discussion also extends to the role of commercial actors and non-independent media outlets in spreading manipulated information. By examining the consequences of these actions on democratic institutions and public trust, the chapter underscores the importance of addressing this issue through enhanced transparency, media literacy, and regulatory measures.

Overview of Political Influence Operations and Manipulation

Political manipulation represents a complex and pressing issue that requires a foundational understanding to fully grasp its impact on democratic processes. Political influence operations are deliberate actions taken by various actors—such as governments, political parties, extremist groups, and private entities—to sway political opinions, decisions, and outcomes. The purpose of these operations often revolves around gaining power, pushing specific agendas, or destabilizing opponents. These tactics can be executed either subtly or overtly, depending on the goals and strategies of those involved.

One of the primary techniques used in political manipulation is disinformation, which involves spreading false or misleading information to deceive the public. This disinformation can come in the form of fake news, manipulated images or videos, and fabricated social media posts designed to look legitimate. By distorting the truth, manipulators aim to influence public perception and create confusion among voters. Another common technique is propaganda, where information is presented in a biased or misleading way to promote a particular political cause or point of view. Propaganda campaigns can be widespread and persistent, often utilizing emotional appeals to sway the audience's opinion.

Astroturfing is another manipulative tactic that creates the illusion of grassroots support for a cause or candidate. This involves orchestrated efforts to make it appear as though thousands of ordinary citizens advocate for a specific agenda, when, in fact, it is being driven by well-funded organizations or individuals. False amplification, where certain messages are artificially boosted through bots and fake accounts to seem more popular than they are, is also prevalent. These methods distort the political discourse and mislead the public about the level of support or opposition for specific policies or candidates.

The agents involved in political manipulation vary widely. Governments, both foreign and domestic, often engage in these activities for different reasons. Foreign governments may manipulate information to influence elections in other countries, advance their own national interests, or simply create chaos and erode trust in democratic institutions. These operations can range from covert activities like cyber attacks and espionage to overt actions such as state-sponsored media campaigns. Domestic governments may also use manipulation tactics to control public opinion, suppress dissent, or marginalize political opponents. Both types of government actors possess significant resources and capabilities, making their influence particularly potent (Arnaudo et al., 2021).

Political parties and campaigns are frequently involved in manipulation efforts, especially during election cycles. They might employ smear campaigns to discredit opponents, utilize targeted advertisements to shape voter perceptions, or even engage in vote tampering. Their main goal is to secure electoral victories, often at any cost. Extremist groups also use manipulation to further their agendas, which may include inciting violence, promoting hate, and increasing political polarization. These groups often target vulnerable populations, exploiting societal divisions to amplify their impact.

Additionally, commercial actors such as private companies, public relations firms, and social media platforms play a role in political manipulation. These entities often operate within the influence industry, providing services that range from managing online reputations to crafting strategic communication plans. In many cases, they collaborate with political campaigns or government agencies to achieve specific objectives. Social media platforms, driven by profit motives, may inadvertently facilitate the spread of disinformation through algorithmic designs that prioritize sensational content over factual information. This dynamic can significantly distort public discourse and fuel misinformation (The Era of Manipulation, n.d.).

Non-independent media outlets, which may be aligned with specific political or economic interests, are also key agents in the manipulation landscape. These media sources might slant their reporting to favor certain narratives or omit critical information that could provide a balanced perspective. The lack of objectivity in such media can misguide the public and contribute to an environment where misinformation thrives. Determining who is behind specific manipulation efforts can be challenging due to overlapping goals and often opaque operations. For example, a foreign state and a domestic political campaign might both benefit from spreading the same piece of disinformation, making attribution difficult.

The impact of political manipulation on democratic processes is profound and multifaceted. One of the most significant effects is the erosion of public trust in democratic institutions. When people are constantly exposed to manipulated information, their confidence in the integrity of elections, the impartiality of the media, and the fairness of governance diminishes. This lack of trust can lead to decreased political participation, as citizens become disillusioned with a system they perceive as corrupt or untrustworthy. Moreover, the spread of disinformation and propaganda can polarize societies, deepen ideological divides, and foster an environment of hostility and intolerance. These divisions weaken the social fabric and make it more challenging to achieve consensus on important issues.

Manipulation efforts can also have direct consequences on election outcomes. By shaping public opinion through deceptive means, manipulators can influence voter behavior and potentially alter the results of elections. This undermines the very essence of democracy, as the will of the people is subverted by hidden forces working behind the scenes. Furthermore, the presence of foreign interference in domestic politics raises concerns about national sovereignty and security. When external actors can meddle in a country's political affairs, it compromises the nation's ability to govern itself independently and according to the wishes of its citizens.

Addressing the challenges posed by political manipulation requires a multifaceted approach. Efforts should focus on enhancing transparency, improving media literacy, and strengthening regulatory frameworks. Transparency initiatives could involve requiring disclosure of funding sources for political advertisements and implementing stricter rules on lobbying activities. Enhancing media literacy among the public can empower individuals to critically evaluate information, identify bias, and recognize manipulation tactics. Additionally, regulatory frameworks must be updated to address the unique challenges posed by digital technologies and social media platforms. This includes holding technology companies accountable for the dissemination of false information and ensuring they implement measures to detect and counteract manipulation efforts.

Examples of Election Interference

Modern democracies face a growing array of tactics aimed at influencing or disrupting elections. These tactics can significantly alter the course of political outcomes, eroding public trust and stability. Understanding these methods is crucial to safeguarding democratic processes.

Case Study of Foreign Interference in Recent Elections

One of the most prominent examples of foreign interference in a recent election occurred during the 2016 United States presidential election. Evidence revealed that Russian actors attempted to sway American voters through various means, including hacking, social media manipulation, and strategic leaks of sensitive information. The U.S. intelligence community asserted that Russia's goals were to undermine public faith in the democratic process, denigrate one candidate, and support another (Election Misinformation | Brennan Center for Justice, n.d.).

The implications of this interference were profound. Not only did it raise questions about the integrity of the electoral system, but it also led to increased political polarization. Similar instances have been documented in other countries, such as the 2017 French presidential election, where Russian-backed hackers targeted the campaign of Emmanuel Macron. These actions demonstrate a sophisticated and coordinated effort to manipulate political outcomes on a global scale.

Techniques Used to Spread Misinformation and Disinformation

Misinformation and disinformation are potent tools used to influence elections. Misinformation refers to false or misleading information spread without malicious intent, while disinformation involves the deliberate dissemination of falsehoods. Both can skew public perception and impact voting behavior.

Common techniques include creating fake news websites, using bots and trolls to amplify misleading content, and hacking into databases to leak selective information. For instance, during the 2020 U.S. presidential election, misinformation about mail-in voting was rampant. False claims that mail-in ballots would lead to widespread voter fraud were propagated across various platforms, despite evidence to the contrary. This narrative contributed to confusion and mistrust among voters (Election Misinformation | Brennan Center for Justice, n.d.).

Another technique involves deepfakes—synthetic media created using artificial intelligence. Deepfakes can create highly realistic yet entirely fabricated audio and video content. These manipulations can mislead voters by making them believe false events or statements are true. As AI technology advances, the threat posed by deepfakes becomes increasingly significant.

Role of Social Media in Election Interference

Social media platforms play a pivotal role in modern election interference. Their vast reach and ability to target specific populations make them ideal tools for those seeking to manipulate opinions. Platforms like Facebook, Twitter, and YouTube have been used to spread both misinformation and disinformation rapidly and widely (Zadrozny, 2024).

During the 2016 Brexit referendum, for example, social media campaigns employed targeted ads to influence voter sentiment. Similarly, during the 2020 U.S. presidential election, social media was flooded with false narratives about voter fraud, leading to real-world actions and protests.

Algorithms that prioritize engagement over accuracy exacerbate the problem. Sensationalist or outrageous content tends to generate more clicks, shares, and comments, which means that misinformation often gets more traction than verified, truthful information. Moreover, the fragmented nature of social media, with echo chambers and filter bubbles, means that individuals are often exposed only to information that reinforces their pre-existing beliefs, making it harder to correct falsehoods.

Consequences of Election Interference on Public Trust and Policy Outcomes

The consequences of election interference extend far beyond individual elections. When the public believes that an election has been tampered with, trust in the entire democratic process can erode. For example, following the 2020 U.S. presidential election, a significant portion of the electorate questioned the legitimacy of the results. This skepticism was fueled by a persistent disinformation campaign claiming that the election had been "stolen" (Zadrozny, 2024).

Such erosion of trust can have long-term implications. Voter turnout may decline as people lose faith in the efficacy of their vote. Additionally, elected officials who are perceived to have benefited from interference may face legitimacy issues, hindering their ability to govern effectively. An environment of distrust can also make it easier for future attempts at interference to succeed, as the public becomes more susceptible to believing in manipulated narratives.

Moreover, the policy outcomes resulting from election interference can be severe. In some cases, policies may be enacted that do not reflect the will of the majority but rather the interests of those behind the interference. For instance, if a candidate supported by foreign entities wins an election, they may feel indebted to those entities, shaping their policy decisions accordingly. This can undermine national sovereignty and compromise the nation's interests.

Lobbying and Its Implications

Lobbying, a profoundly influential activity within political systems, is an attempt to sway government action through direct interaction with lawmakers. Historically, lobbying has roots tracing back to ancient democracies where citizens would petition their leaders for various causes. In the modern era, lobbying has evolved into a complex and multifaceted practice, often executed by professional advocates, corporations, and special interest groups.

Lobbying involves a range of tactics designed to influence legislation. One common tactic is face-to-face meetings with lawmakers, where lobbyists present arguments and evidence supporting their positions. These interactions may include providing data, research findings, or case studies that highlight the benefits of a proposed legislative change. Another tactic is grassroots lobbying, where lobbyists mobilize public opinion to pressure legislators by organizing calls, emails, and social media campaigns. Additionally, financial contributions to political campaigns are a means through which lobbyists gain access and favor with policymakers.

The ethical and legal boundaries of lobbying practices are crucial aspects to consider in understanding its impact on political systems. Lobbying is legally protected under the First Amendment in the United States, which grants individuals and groups the right to petition the government. Furthermore, regulations such as the Lobbying Disclosure Act of 1995 require lobbyists to register and report their activities, ensuring transparency and accountability. However, ethical concerns arise when lobbying intersects with undue influence and potential corruption. For instance, the fine line between lobbying and bribery becomes blurred when substantial gifts or favors are involved. In these cases, distinguishing legitimate advocacy from unethical conduct is essential for maintaining the integrity of democratic processes.

The effects of lobbying on legislation and public perception are profound and multifaceted. On one hand, lobbying can enhance the legislative process by providing lawmakers with valuable information and expertise. For example, industry specialists can offer insights that help shape informed policy decisions, benefiting both legislators and constituents. Economist Thomas Sowell highlights this beneficial aspect, stating, "Reform through democratic legislation requires either public consensus or a powerful minority lobby." This underscores how lobbying can facilitate necessary reforms and encourage participatory democracy.

Conversely, the dominance of well-funded lobbying groups can skew the legislative agenda, favoring interests over the broader public good. When powerful entities monopolize lawmakers' attention, critical issues affecting marginalized or less affluent communities may be sidelined. For instance, environmental policies can be heavily influenced by corporate lobbying from industries prioritizing economic gains over ecological sustainability. The perception that policymakers are more responsive to lobbyists than ordinary citizens can erode public trust in government institutions.

Lobbying's role in shaping public perception cannot be underestimated. Media coverage of lobbying efforts and the portrayal of lobbyists in popular culture significantly color public attitudes toward the practice. When lobbying actions align with broadly supported causes, they can garner favorable public opinion, showcasing the positive impact of organized advocacy. Conversely, high-profile scandals involving unethical lobbying practices can reinforce negative stereotypes, portraying lobbyists as manipulators undermining democratic ideals.

To maintain a balanced and fair political system, it is essential to address the challenges associated with lobbying. Striking a balance between allowing free speech and preventing undue influence is key. Tightening regulations and enforcing existing laws can mitigate the risks of corrupt practices while promoting transparency. Public financing of political campaigns and stringent caps on contributions can reduce lawmakers' dependency on lobbyist-provided funds, leveling the playing field for all interest groups.

Moreover, educating citizens about the role and impact of lobbying can democratize the process. By fostering awareness and encouraging civic engagement, individuals are better equipped to participate in advocacy efforts, ensuring that diverse voices contribute to the legislative narrative. Initiatives like town hall meetings, public hearings, and online platforms for citizen feedback can bridge the gap between lawmakers and constituents, counterbalancing the concentrated influence of professional lobbyists.

Corruption in Political Systems

Political manipulation is a multifaceted issue with deep repercussions for the integrity of political systems around the world. One significant aspect that erodes such integrity is corruption. This subpoint will delve into the various forms of corruption, offer high-profile case studies from around the globe, discuss its economic and social costs, and present strategies to combat this pervasive problem.

Definition and Types of Political Corruption

Political corruption can be defined as the abuse of public power for private gain. This broad definition encompasses numerous forms of corrupt activities. Some common types include bribery, nepotism, embezzlement, and patronage. Bribery involves offering something valuable to influence the actions of an official. Nepotism occurs when officials show favoritism toward family members in their appointments or decisions. Embezzlement refers to the theft of public resources by officials entrusted with their management. Patronage is the granting of favors, contracts, or appointments to political supporters rather than based on merit.

The boundary of what constitutes corruption can vary across cultures. In some societies, behaviors viewed as permissible might be regarded as corrupt in others (Wei, 2001). For instance, a survey in Thailand revealed a higher tolerance for certain governmental behaviors compared to Western nations. Nevertheless, extreme abuses of power are universally condemned and pose significant risks to macroeconomic stability (Wei, 2001).

High-Profile Cases of Political Corruption Globally

Numerous cases of political corruption have made headlines worldwide. One notable example is the Watergate scandal in the United States, where illegal activities led to the resignation of President Richard Nixon. Another high-profile case is the "Lava Jato" or Operation Car Wash investigation in Brazil, which uncovered a massive corruption scheme involving Petrobras, the state-controlled oil company, and numerous politicians and executives.

In South Africa, former President Jacob Zuma faced charges related to a sprawling corruption scandal that included allegations of bribes paid by wealthy businessmen for political favors. Similarly, in India, the 2G spectrum scam involved government officials who allegedly accepted kickbacks for undervaluing telecom licenses, costing the government billions in potential revenue. These examples highlight that corruption is not confined to any one region but is a global issue undermining political integrity.

The Economic and Social Costs of Corruption

Corruption has far-reaching economic and social consequences. Economically, it acts as an impediment to growth and development. Countries with high levels of corruption tend to attract less foreign direct investment (FDI), crucial for industrialization and development. Research shows that corruption can act similarly to a heavy tax burden, discouraging investments without generating public revenue (Wei, 2001).

Corruption also diverts public resources away from essential services like healthcare, education, and infrastructure, leading to inefficiencies and poor service delivery. It stifles innovation and competition, as businesses may find it more profitable to engage in corrupt practices rather than improving their offerings. Moreover, it raises the costs of goods and services as companies often pass the cost of bribes onto consumers.

Socially, corruption erodes trust in public institutions and diminishes citizen engagement in democratic processes. People become disillusioned when they perceive that their leaders are more interested in personal gain than public service. This lack of trust can lead to increased political instability and, in extreme cases, civil unrest.

Strategies for Combating Corruption in Political Systems

Combating corruption requires a comprehensive approach that includes legal, institutional, and societal measures. Effective anti-corruption strategies involve both preventive and punitive actions. Below are several strategies that have been successfully implemented in various contexts:

1. **Strengthening Legal Frameworks**: Laws specifically targeting corruption are essential. These should cover all forms of corruption and include stringent penalties for offenders. Additionally, laws promoting transparency and accountability, such as freedom of information acts, can be effective.

2. **Establishing Independent Anti-Corruption Bodies**: Institutions dedicated to fighting corruption can play a crucial role. These bodies should be independent from political influence, well-resourced, and empowered to investigate and prosecute corruption cases. Examples include the Independent Commission Against Corruption (ICAC) in Hong Kong and Transparency International, which plays a vital role in fighting corruption globally.

3. **Enhancing Public Sector Accountability**: Public sector reforms aimed at increasing accountability can significantly reduce opportunities for corruption. This includes implementing transparent procurement procedures, regular audits of public finances, and merit-based recruitment and promotion in public services.

4. **Promoting Citizen Engagement and Awareness**: Educating citizens about their rights and the importance of integrity in governance can foster a culture of accountability. Civil society organizations and media play a key role in monitoring government actions and holding officials accountable. Whistleblower protection laws are also critical to encourage reporting of corrupt activities without fear of retaliation.

5. **Leveraging Technology**: Technology can be a powerful tool against corruption. E-governance initiatives, where government services are provided online, reduce direct interaction between citizens and officials, thereby minimizing opportunities for bribery. Blockchain technology is another emerging tool that can

enhance transparency and traceability in governmental transactions.

6. **International Cooperation**: Corruption is often transnational, requiring international cooperation for effective enforcement. Agreements like the United Nations Convention Against Corruption (UNCAC) provide a framework for countries to collaborate in preventing and combating corruption.

Exploitation of Political Processes by Foreign and Domestic Entities

The exploitation of political systems by both foreign and domestic actors is a multifaceted issue with significant implications for national security and sovereignty. This subpoint delves into the various methods employed by these actors to influence political outcomes, highlighting the vulnerabilities within our systems and offering strategies for mitigation.

Foreign entities often utilize sophisticated techniques to sway political outcomes in other nations. One prominent method is cyber espionage, where state-sponsored hackers infiltrate government networks to steal sensitive information or manipulate data. Such activities can compromise election processes, as seen in recent incidents where foreign hackers targeted voter databases and electoral infrastructure. For example, the Russian Foreign Intelligence Service (SVR) has been known to exploit software vulnerabilities to gain access to critical systems globally (Russian Cyber Actors Are Exploiting a Known Vulnerability with Worldwide Impact, n.d.). By doing so, they can disseminate misinformation, undermine public trust, and potentially alter election results.

Apart from cyber espionage, foreign powers also engage in propaganda and disinformation campaigns. They use social media platforms to spread false narratives and divisive content, aiming to polarize societies and create discord. These campaigns are often designed to amplify existing tensions within a country, thus weakening its social fabric. The impact of such operations on democratic processes cannot be overstated, as they erode the public's confidence in their institutions and leaders.

On the domestic front, various actors exploit loopholes and weaknesses within the political system to further their agendas. One common tactic is the manipulation of electoral boundaries through gerrymandering. By redrawing district lines to favor a particular party, politicians can effectively rig elections, ensuring that their party remains in power regardless of the popular vote. This practice undermines the principles of fair representation and distorts the will of the electorate.

Another method of domestic exploitation involves the use of dark money in politics. By funneling large sums of untraceable funds into political campaigns, wealthy individuals and special interest groups can exert undue influence over elected officials. This financial power can shape policy decisions, as politicians may feel beholden to their donors rather than their constituents. The lack of transparency in campaign financing thus poses a significant threat to the integrity of the political system.

The exploitation of political systems by both foreign and domestic actors has profound implications for national security and sovereignty. When external forces meddle in a country's political affairs, it can lead to a loss of control over domestic policies and decision-making. For instance, if a foreign power manages to install sympathetic leaders through covert operations, it could steer the country's foreign policy in a direction that benefits the meddling nation rather than the host country. This undermines the principle of self-determination and can result in unfavorable diplomatic or economic arrangements.

Domestically, the erosion of public trust in institutions due to political manipulation can have far-reaching consequences. When citizens believe that their electoral system is rigged or that their leaders are corrupt, they may become disillusioned with democracy itself. This disillusionment can lead to lower voter turnout, increased civil unrest, and a rise in extremist movements. Ultimately, the stability of the nation is at risk when its political foundation is compromised.

To counter these threats and protect the integrity of political systems, several mitigation strategies must be put in place. First and foremost, robust cybersecurity measures are essential to defend against foreign cyber threats. Governments and private organizations must collaborate to identify vulnerabilities, share intelligence, and implement best practices for protecting critical infrastructure. Regular audits and updates to security protocols can help stay ahead of potential attackers.

Additionally, promoting transparency in political financing is crucial. Implementing stringent disclosure requirements for campaign contributions and expenditures can curb the influence of dark money. Publicly funded campaigns or matching funds programs can also reduce candidates' reliance on wealthy donors, leveling the playing field and ensuring that elected officials remain accountable to their constituents.

Legal reforms are necessary to address domestic exploitation tactics such as gerrymandering. Independent redistricting commissions, composed of non-partisan members, can oversee the drawing of electoral boundaries, ensuring that districts are created fairly and reflect true demographic patterns. This can help restore public confidence in the democratic process and ensure that all votes carry equal weight.

Educating the public about the dangers of disinformation is another vital strategy. Media literacy programs can equip citizens with the skills to critically evaluate news sources and identify fake news. By fostering an informed and discerning electorate, societies can become more resilient to manipulation attempts. Social media platforms also bear responsibility in this regard and should take proactive measures to identify and remove fake accounts and misleading content.

Finally, strengthening international cooperation is key to combating the global nature of political exploitation. Nations must work together to establish norms and agreements that prevent interference in each other's internal affairs. Diplomatic efforts can include sanctions against countries that engage in political manipulation and support for multilateral initiatives aimed at safeguarding democratic processes worldwide.

This chapter provided an in-depth exploration of how various actors employ political influence operations to manipulate processes and decisions within democratic systems. We examined the techniques used, including disinformation, propaganda, astroturfing, and false amplification, all designed to distort the truth and sway public opinion. The chapter also detailed the roles played by different agents such as governments, political parties, extremist groups, private companies, and non-independent media in these manipulative efforts. Additionally, it highlighted the significant impact of these operations on democratic institutions, fostering public distrust, polarization, and diminishing electoral integrity.

In understanding the strategies and actors involved in political manipulation, we gain insight into the profound challenges faced by modern democracies. The discussion underscored the need for transparency, media literacy, and robust regulatory frameworks to counteract these tactics effectively. Addressing these complex issues requires a multifaceted approach that includes legal measures, public education, and cooperation among nations to safeguard democratic processes. By recognizing the depth and reach of political manipulation, societies can work towards strengthening their resilience against these disruptive forces, ensuring a more informed and engaged electorate.

Chapter 5

Security Breaches

Security breaches pose significant risks to both individuals and organizations, creating vulnerabilities that can have far-reaching consequences. These breaches can occur through various methods, each with the potential to disrupt operations, compromise sensitive data, and erode trust. The chapter delves into the multifaceted nature of security breaches, examining how they manifest in different forms and the extensive implications they hold for national security, economic stability, and diplomatic relations.

In this chapter, readers will explore diverse real-world examples illustrating the impact of security breaches. From historical espionage activities to contemporary cyber warfare, these case studies provide a comprehensive understanding of the evolving tactics used by malicious actors. The discussion also highlights insider threats and the critical role they play in compromising security from within. By analyzing these scenarios, the chapter underscores the necessity for robust security measures, comprehensive employee training, and international cooperation to mitigate the risks associated with security breaches.

Examination of espionage activities targeting national security

Espionage, in its essence, is an activity conducted by governments or corporate entities to obtain confidential information without the permission of the holder. This clandestine practice has existed throughout history and continues to evolve with technological advancements. The primary objective of espionage is to acquire valuable intelligence that can provide a strategic advantage over adversaries. Understanding how espionage operates helps in comprehending the significant threat it poses to national security.

Historically, espionage has been a pivotal tool in international relations and conflicts. During the Cold War, for instance, espionage activities between the United States and the Soviet Union were rampant. Both superpowers employed a range of espionage methods to gather crucial intelligence on each other's military capabilities, political strategies, and technological developments. This period saw numerous spy agencies come into prominence, such as the CIA in the United States and the KGB in the Soviet Union. These organizations engaged in covert operations, recruitment of informants, and use of advanced surveillance equipment to meet their intelligence-gathering goals.

In contemporary times, espionage methods have become increasingly sophisticated, leveraging modern technology to enhance the efficiency and reach of spying activities. Cyber espionage is one of the most prevalent forms today, involving the use of digital tools to infiltrate computer systems and networks of target states or corporations. Hackers can extract sensitive data, monitor communications, and disrupt operations with relative anonymity and minimal physical risk. Notable cyber espionage incidents include China's alleged theft of intellectual property from Western companies and Russia's hacking activities targeting political entities in various countries (Nation-State Cyber Espionage and Its Impacts, 2013).

Satellite surveillance also plays a critical role in modern espionage. Satellites equipped with high-resolution cameras and other sensing devices provide unparalleled observation capabilities. They can capture detailed images of military installations, track movements of troops and equipment, and even intercept communications signals. This form of remote sensing enables continuous monitoring of strategic locations across the globe, contributing significantly to a nation's intelligence capabilities.

Human Intelligence (HUMINT) remains an indispensable aspect of espionage despite advancements in technology. HUMINT involves the recruitment and management of spies who can provide firsthand information on the inner workings of adversary governments or organizations. These agents often operate in highly secretive environments, gathering intelligence through direct access to key personnel or by infiltrating sensitive areas. The value of HUMINT lies in its ability to offer nuanced insights that technical means may not capture, such as motivations, intentions, and human behavior.

The consequences of espionage on national integrity are profound and far-reaching. One of the most immediate impacts is the compromise of military secrets. Espionage can expose information about defense strategies, weapons systems, and operational plans, putting a nation at a significant disadvantage in potential conflicts. For example, during World War II, Nazi spies attempted to uncover the secrets behind American aviation technology, which could have altered the course of the war if successful (<i>Economic Espionage</i>, n.d.).

Economic losses are another significant consequence of espionage. When foreign entities steal trade secrets, intellectual property, or proprietary technologies, it undermines the economic competitiveness of the targeted nation. This theft can lead to financial losses for affected companies, reduced investment in innovation, and job displacement. Economic espionage is a long-term threat to a nation's prosperity, as it erodes the foundation of industries that drive growth and development.

Diplomatic tensions are often exacerbated by espionage activities. When instances of spying are exposed, they can lead to strained relations between nations. Accusations of espionage can result in diplomatic fallout, including the expulsion of diplomats, imposition of sanctions, or breakdowns in bilateral cooperation. For example, the revelation of U.S. surveillance programs by Edward Snowden in 2013 caused significant diplomatic friction between the United States and its allies.

Impact of cyber warfare, espionage, and insider threats

Cyber activities and internal threats pose significant risks to modern security frameworks. As cyber warfare continues to evolve, it has become increasingly adept at disrupting critical infrastructure through sophisticated hacking techniques and malware attacks. One notable example is the Stuxnet worm, an advanced piece of malware designed to target Iran's nuclear facilities. This attack demonstrated how a strategically deployed cyber weapon could cause physical damage to infrastructure, leading to widespread operational disruptions.

Another prominent instance of cyber warfare is the alleged Russian interference in the 2016 U.S. elections. Through a series of coordinated cyber activities, including phishing, data breaches, and misinformation campaigns, malicious actors aimed to undermine the integrity of the electoral process. The implications of this interference were profound, raising questions about the security of democratic systems and the potential for future electoral manipulation.

The SolarWinds hack further illustrates the scale and impact of cyber breaches. In this incident, attackers infiltrated the software supply chain of SolarWinds, a major IT management company, compromising several government agencies and private sector organizations. The breach remained undetected for months, allowing the attackers to exfiltrate sensitive data and gather intelligence on a massive scale. This event underscored the vulnerabilities inherent in interconnected digital environments and highlighted the urgent need for robust cybersecurity measures.

While external cyber threats are a formidable challenge, insider threats represent an equally daunting risk to security. Employees or contractors with authorized access to sensitive information can exploit their positions for personal or financial gain, intentionally or unintentionally causing harm to the organization. Insider threats often go unnoticed until the damage is done, making them particularly insidious.

High-profile cases such as Edward Snowden's leak of National Security Agency (NSA) documents exemplify the devastating impact of insider threats. Snowden, a former NSA contractor, disclosed classified information on global surveillance programs, sparking international controversy and damaging diplomatic relations. This incident underscored the necessity of stringent insider threat programs to detect and prevent unauthorized disclosures.

To mitigate the risks posed by both cyber activities and internal threats, organizations must adopt comprehensive security strategies. Implementing stringent access controls is a crucial first step. Access to sensitive information should be restricted based on the principle of least privilege, where employees are granted only the minimum access necessary to perform their duties. Regular audits and reviews of access permissions can help identify and address any discrepancies, further bolstering security.

In addition to access controls, robust cybersecurity measures are essential for protecting against external threats. Organizations should invest in advanced threat detection and prevention tools, such as intrusion detection systems (IDS) and intrusion prevention systems (IPS). These technologies can identify suspicious activity in real time and respond accordingly to thwart potential attacks.

Continuous monitoring is another vital component of an effective security strategy. By maintaining constant vigilance over network traffic and user behaviors, organizations can identify anomalies that may indicate a security breach or insider threat. Behavioral analytics, which analyze patterns of user activity to detect deviations from normal behavior, can provide early warnings of potential issues. This proactive approach enables swift intervention before an incident escalates.

Training and awareness programs are also crucial for mitigating insider threats. Educating employees about the importance of security and the potential consequences of policy violations can foster a culture of vigilance and responsibility. Regular training sessions should cover topics such as recognizing phishing attempts, reporting suspicious activity, and adhering to data handling protocols. Encouraging a sense of ownership and accountability among employees can significantly reduce the likelihood of insider threats materializing.

Organizations should also establish clear procedures for reporting and responding to security incidents. A well-defined incident response plan ensures that all stakeholders understand their roles and responsibilities in the event of a breach. Timely and coordinated responses are critical for minimizing the impact of security incidents and restoring normal operations as quickly as possible.

Collaboration with external partners is another key aspect of a robust security strategy. Sharing threat intelligence with industry peers and government agencies can enhance situational awareness and improve collective defenses. Participating in information-sharing initiatives and collaborating on best practices can help organizations stay ahead of emerging threats and develop more effective mitigation strategies.

Case studies of security breaches and their consequences

The impact of security breaches on global scales can be vividly illustrated through notable case studies that highlight the severe repercussions and lessons learned from these incidents.

One of the most significant cases is Edward Snowden's leak of NSA documents in 2013, which had far-reaching global repercussions. Snowden, a former contractor at the National Security Agency, disclosed thousands of classified documents revealing the extent of the NSA's surveillance activities. This included the collection of phone records and internet communications of millions of people worldwide without their knowledge or consent (Greenwald et al., 2013). The leak sparked a global debate about privacy, government surveillance, and data security. Public opinion was divided; some viewed Snowden as a whistleblower exposing government overreach, while others saw him as a traitor compromising national security. The disclosures led to significant changes in legislation and policies aimed at increasing transparency and protecting individual privacy. Nonetheless, they also strained international relations, particularly between the United States and its allies.

Another critical example is the Office of Personnel Management (OPM) data breach, which exposed the personal information of approximately 21.5 million current and former federal employees, including security clearance information. Discovered in 2015, this breach raised serious concerns about identity theft and national security vulnerabilities. The stolen data included Social Security numbers, fingerprints, and background investigation details, making those affected prime targets for identity fraud and espionage (Geiger, 2018). The implications of this breach underscored the importance of safeguarding sensitive information and implementing robust cybersecurity measures within government agencies. In response, the OPM undertook extensive efforts to improve its security protocols, including the adoption of multi-factor authentication and enhanced network monitoring.

The Sony Pictures hack in 2014 serves as another stark reminder of the potential damage resulting from security breaches. Hackers infiltrated Sony's computer systems, releasing confidential emails, employee information, and unreleased films. This incident had a profound impact on both corporate and entertainment sectors. Financial losses were incurred due to disrupted operations and damage control efforts. Creative projects were jeopardized as leaked information included detailed plans for future film releases, leading to significant financial and reputational setbacks for Sony Pictures. Moreover, the breach revealed internal communications that strained professional relationships and damaged the company's public image. The hack was attributed to a group linked to North Korea, allegedly in retaliation for the planned release of a satirical film about the North Korean leader. This highlighted the geopolitical dimensions of cyber warfare and the vulnerabilities even large corporations face against state-sponsored attacks.

From these case studies, several critical lessons emerge that underscore the necessity of robust security protocols, comprehensive employee training, and international cooperation. Firstly, implementing stringent security measures is vital in protecting sensitive information from unauthorized access. Organizations must regularly update their cybersecurity practices, conduct vulnerability assessments, and ensure compliance with industry standards. Secondly, training employees to recognize and respond to potential threats is essential in preventing breaches caused by human error. Educating staff about phishing scams, secure password management, and the importance of reporting suspicious activities can significantly reduce the risk of internal threats. Lastly, international cooperation is crucial in addressing cybersecurity challenges that transcend national borders. Governments and organizations must collaborate on sharing intelligence, developing unified response strategies, and establishing norms for responsible behavior in cyberspace.

Reflection

In this chapter, we explored the multifaceted nature of security breaches, discussing both historical and modern approaches to espionage. We delved into how espionage has evolved with technological advancements, highlighting forms such as cyber and satellite surveillance alongside traditional human intelligence methods. The real-world examples provided, from

Cold War espionage to contemporary cyber threats like the SolarWinds hack, illustrated the profound implications of these activities on national integrity, economic stability, and diplomatic relations.

Furthermore, the chapter underscored the necessity for robust security measures in mitigating the risks posed by espionage and cyber warfare. By examining case studies such as Edward Snowden's leaks and the OPM data breach, we recognized critical lessons in enhancing security protocols, training employees, and fostering international cooperation. These insights stress the importance of vigilance, technology-driven defenses, and collaborative efforts to safeguard against the ever-evolving landscape of security threats.

Chapter 6

Legal and Judicial Challenges

Legal and judicial challenges present intricate issues that deeply affect national sovereignty. These challenges can arise from the inherent vulnerabilities within legal systems, such as exploitation of procedural gaps, corruption, and legislative loopholes. Furthermore, the influence of political power over judicial decisions complicates the impartiality essential for a fair justice system. Through this chapter, we aim to explore these multifaceted aspects, shedding light on how they disrupt legal integrity and public trust.

The chapter delves into specific areas impacted by legal and judicial challenges. It begins with an examination of primary legal vulnerabilities, including procedural manipulations and the misuse of legal loopholes. This is followed by a discussion on the detrimental effects of corruption within judicial processes. The chapter also analyzes how ambiguous or outdated legislation creates opportunities for exploitation. Moreover, it highlights the implications of political interference in judicial decisions, demonstrating the adverse effects on judicial independence and democratic governance. By addressing these elements, the chapter provides a comprehensive understanding of the complexities and ramifications of legal and judicial challenges on national sovereignty.

Exploration of Legal Vulnerabilities

Understanding the primary legal vulnerabilities and threats to the rule of law is paramount in safeguarding national sovereignty. One of the foremost concerns is identifying key areas where legal systems are prone to exploitation. Legal systems, regardless of their robustness, often harbor points of vulnerability that can be manipulated by those seeking to undermine justice. These exploitations can range from procedural manipulations during trials to the misuse of legal loopholes that allow wrongful acquittals or unjust dismissals of cases. Such weaknesses not only hinder the delivery of justice but also erode public confidence in legal institutions.

Corruption poses a significant threat to the integrity of judicial processes. When corruption infiltrates judiciary corridors, it morphs legal systems into mechanisms of oppression rather than pillars of justice. Bribery, nepotism, and undue influence lead to biased verdicts, further entrenching inequality and disenfranchising the vulnerable. Studies have shown that countries with high levels of judicial corruption struggle with prolonged court cases and inconsistent rulings, emphasizing the urgent need for reform (*Rule of Law | Democracy, Human Rights and Governance*, 2022).

An analysis of loopholes in legislation reveals how these gaps undermine legal enforcement. Loopholes often exist due to ambiguous wording, outdated laws that fail to address contemporary issues, or intentional omissions crafted to benefit powerful entities. For instance, cybercrime laws lag behind the rapid evolution of technology, leaving digital offenses inadequately penalized. Similarly, environmental regulations might be rife with exceptions that large corporations exploit to bypass stringent pollution controls. Addressing these loopholes requires a continuous process of legislative review and modernization to ensure comprehensive legal coverage.

The influence of political power over legal decisions is another critical area of concern. When political forces exert undue influence on judicial proceedings, it disrupts the balance of power central to democratic governance. Judges may face pressure to deliver verdicts favoring the government or influential political figures, thereby compromising judicial independence. This politicization of justice can manifest in various forms, such as appointing judges based on political loyalty rather than merit, manipulating case assignments, or using legal tools to target political opponents. Upholding the principle of judicial independence is essential to maintaining the sanctity of the rule of law and ensuring that the judiciary remains an impartial arbiter of justice.

Corruption in judicial processes demonstrates the devastating impact on equitable justice provision. A corrupt judiciary prioritizes personal gain over public service, leading to skewed decisions that favor the affluent and connected. The access to fair trial becomes a privilege rather than a right, deepening social divides and breeding widespread disillusionment with legal institutions. Countries grappling with systemic judicial corruption often experience lower foreign investment and increased civil unrest as citizens lose faith in their ability to seek redress through lawful means.

Loopholes in legislation offer fertile ground for exploitation, undermining efforts to enforce law consistently and fairly. Criminals and corporate entities adept at navigating these gaps can evade liability, emboldening others to follow suit. Legislative loopholes can also hamper international cooperation in combating transnational crimes like human trafficking, money laundering, and terrorism financing. Streamlining laws to close these gaps is imperative to fortify legal frameworks against exploitation.

Political power's sway over legal decisions brings forth a litany of issues detrimental to the rule of law. The instrumentalization of law for political ends destabilizes trust in governmental fairness and neutrality. It leads to a climate of fear among judicial officers who might resort to self-censorship or bias to avoid repercussions. Political interference often results in selective justice, where allies are shielded from prosecution while detractors are disproportionately targeted. Ensuring that judiciaries operate free of partisan pressures is vital for preserving democracy and justice.

Efforts to bolster the rule of law must address these vulnerabilities head-on. Anti-corruption measures, including transparent appointment processes, rigorous audits, and robust whistleblower protections, can mitigate the corrosive effects of judicial corruption. Strengthening international cooperation and adopting global standards can help close legislative loopholes, ensuring consistent enforcement across borders. Promoting judicial independence through constitutional safeguards, professional development, and public oversight can shield legal systems from political machinations.

International Lawfare and Regulatory Capture

International lawfare, a term increasingly gaining attention, refers to the strategy of using legal systems and principles to achieve military or political objectives. Unlike traditional warfare, which utilizes physical force, lawfare involves leveraging international and domestic laws to weaken an adversary's position. One prevalent tactic within international lawfare is the filing of lawsuits in international courts to challenge the actions of a state or its officials. For instance, smaller nations may bring cases against more powerful states in international tribunals to gain diplomatic leverage. Additionally, there have been instances where organizations utilize human rights laws to constrain military operations by alleging violations that bring global scrutiny and pressure.

Foreign entities often use legal measures to influence domestic policies, thereby exerting considerable impact on national sovereignty. These entities can include other countries, multinational corporations, or international organizations. They may engage in extensive lobbying within another country's legal system, pushing for changes that align with their interests. An example of this is when multinational corporations lobby for favorable trade regulations or intellectual property laws that benefit them but may not necessarily align with the host country's best interests. Another tactic includes utilizing bilateral investment treaties (BITs) to challenge unfavorable policy decisions through arbitration panels, which can result in significant financial awards against the concerned nation.

Regulatory capture presents another dimension of legal challenges impacting governance and policy-making. This phenomenon occurs when regulatory agencies, established to act in the public's interest, end up being dominated by the industries they are supposed to regulate. Essentially, the regulators start to serve the interests of the businesses they oversee instead of safeguarding the public good. A classic example of regulatory capture is observed in the financial sector, where large banks exert significant influence over regulatory bodies, leading to lax regulations that contributed to economic crises. Similarly, in the energy sector, substantial lobbying efforts by fossil fuel companies can impede the development and implementation of robust environmental regulations, thereby affecting climate policies and public health.

Examining successful and unsuccessful instances of lawfare provides deeper insights into its practical implications. A notable case of successful lawfare is the use of the International Criminal Court (ICC) by countries to hold foreign leaders accountable for war crimes and human rights abuses. The ICC has issued warrants against several high-profile individuals, creating international pressure and sometimes leading to changes in leadership or policy. Conversely, there have been unsuccessful attempts, such as when certain nations try to use international environmental laws to halt infrastructure projects in other countries. These attempts may fail due to insufficient legal grounds or the defending country's diplomatic maneuvers, illustrating the complexities and limitations inherent in lawfare.

Legal Challenges and Impacts on Sovereignty

Understanding the complexities of legal battles and their impact on national sovereignty is crucial in navigating the ever-evolving landscape of international relations. National borders, natural resources, trade disputes, and supranational courts all play significant roles in shaping a nation's sovereignty. To delve deeper into this topic, we'll examine several landmark legal cases that have had profound effects on national sovereignty.

One of the most notable cases involving national borders is the dispute between the United States and Mexico over the Rio Grande. This case highlights how legal battles can shape national boundaries and influence diplomatic relations. Historically, the border between the two countries was defined by the river's course. However, natural changes in the river's course led to conflicting claims over territories, resulting in persistent legal disputes. The 1963 Chamizal Treaty resolved one such dispute, realigning the border and compensating affected landowners. This case underscores the importance of legal mechanisms in resolving territorial disagreements and maintaining peaceful international relations.

Beyond territorial disputes, legal battles over natural resources have significant geopolitical implications. The South China Sea conflict exemplifies this. Multiple nations, including China, Vietnam, the Philippines, Malaysia, and Brunei, claim parts of this resource-rich region. In 2016, an arbitration tribunal constituted under the United Nations Convention on the Law of the Sea (UNCLOS) ruled against China's expansive claims. Despite the ruling, China continued its activities in the region, demonstrating the complexities of enforcing international legal decisions. This ongoing dispute underscores the challenge of balancing legal rulings with geopolitical strategies and the importance of international law in managing resource-related conflicts.

International trade disputes also play a crucial role in shaping national sovereignty. One prominent example is the longstanding trade conflict between the United States and China. This trade war has involved numerous legal battles over tariffs, intellectual property rights, and market access. The World Trade Organization (WTO) has been instrumental in adjudicating some of these disputes, highlighting the economic consequences of legal challenges in international trade. These disputes not only affect the economies of the involved countries but also influence global trade patterns and relationships. For instance, the imposition of tariffs can lead to retaliation, affecting various industries and leading to shifts in global supply chains.

Supranational courts play an increasingly important role in enforcing decisions against sovereign states, further complicating the relationship between national sovereignty and international law. Institutions like the International Court of Justice (ICJ) and the European Court of Human Rights (ECHR) are pivotal in this regard. A prime example is the ICJ's ruling in the case between Nicaragua and Colombia over maritime boundaries in the Caribbean Sea. The 2012 ruling adjusted the maritime boundaries, granting more territorial waters to Nicaragua. While Colombia initially rejected the decision, it eventually acknowledged the ruling, illustrating both the power and limitations of supranational courts in enforcing international law.

The European Union provides another poignant example of the influence of supranational courts. The European Court of Justice (ECJ) has made multiple rulings impacting the sovereignty of EU member states. Cases such as the ECJ's decision on privacy rights in the Digital Rights Ireland case, which invalidated the EU Data Retention Directive, showcase how supranational legal decisions can directly impact national legislation and policies. Such rulings emphasize that while supranational courts aim to create a unified legal framework, they can also generate tensions between national laws and broader regional regulations.

Implications for Rule of Law

To analyze how legal challenges impact the overall rule of law within a nation, one must first understand how these challenges can erode public trust in judicial systems. Legal systems are foundational to the contract between a government and its citizens; when they are perceived as unreliable or unjust, public confidence wanes. Legal disputes that appear biased or politically motivated undermine the judiciary's independence, creating a sense of disenfranchisement among the populace. This erosion of trust is particularly concerning as it can lead to civil unrest and reduced compliance with legal directives, which in turn weakens the rule of law itself.

For instance, when judges are seen as partial or corrupt, people lose faith in fair trials and due process. According to the United Nations, strengthening the rule of law involves ensuring public services are accessible and corruption is curbed (United Nations, 2015). Without this trust, a society struggles to function cohesively, and the rule of law becomes more theoretical than practical. Media plays a critical role in either supporting or undermining this trust, as it shapes public perception through its coverage of judicial proceedings and legal challenges (The Global Assault on Rule of Law, n.d.). A balanced and unbiased media is essential for maintaining public confidence in legal systems, thereby preserving their integrity.

Another significant aspect revolves around the delicate balance between security measures and civil liberties. In times of national crisis or threats to security, governments often adopt strict measures to protect citizens. However, these measures can sometimes infringe upon individual freedoms. For example, extensive surveillance programs may be justified as necessary for national security but can also be viewed as violations of personal privacy. Striking a balance between maintaining safety and upholding civil liberties is crucial. Overemphasis on security at the cost of liberty can trigger public dissent, thus destabilizing governance structures and diminishing respect for the law. Conversely, insufficient security measures may render a state vulnerable to threats, further complicating the governance landscape.

Legal uncertainties also have a profound effect on business environments and investments. Investors seek stable, predictable legal frameworks within which to operate. Uncertainties such as inconsistent application of laws, arbitrary changes in regulations, or prolonged legal disputes deter both domestic and foreign investment. Businesses require certainty to plan for the future, allocate resources effectively, and manage risks. When legal systems are plagued by ambiguity and inefficiency, it undermines economic activities and stunts growth. The administrative burden and financial costs associated with navigating uncertain legal terrains can be prohibitive, deterring new ventures and innovation. Clear and consistent legal frameworks are therefore essential for fostering a conducive business environment that attracts investment and promotes economic prosperity.

To withstand external and internal pressures, nations should consider strategies for strengthening their legal frameworks. One effective approach is the development of inclusive and accountable justice systems. According to the United Nations, an inclusive system ensures that all individuals, regardless of background, have equal access to justice (United Nations, 2015). This inclusivity boosts public confidence and fortifies the rule of law. Additionally, legal reforms aimed at increasing transparency and reducing corruption are vital. Implementing stringent anti-corruption laws and establishing independent bodies to oversee judicial conduct can help build a more robust legal framework.

Educational initiatives are another crucial strategy. Public education about the importance of the rule of law, the functioning of the judiciary, and the rights and responsibilities of citizens fosters a more informed and engaged populace. Civic education strengthens societal support for judicial systems and promotes active participation in democratic processes. According to sources, better civic education can counteract the view that the judiciary hampers democratic rule, thereby promoting respect for constitutional values (The Global Assault on Rule of Law, n.d.).

Moreover, the international community can provide technical assistance to help nations develop stronger legal infrastructures. Collaborative efforts between countries and international organizations can share best practices and resources, aiding in the establishment of resilient legal systems. International guidelines and conventions also play a role in harmonizing legal standards, contributing to greater consistency and predictability in global legal practices.

This chapter delves into the intricate interplay between legal challenges and their profound impact on national sovereignty. By examining vulnerabilities within legal systems, such as procedural manipulations, corruption, and legislative loopholes, we uncover how these weaknesses can erode trust and equity in justice. The influence of political power over judicial decisions further complicates this landscape, stressing the need for robust reforms to uphold the integrity and independence of legal institutions.

Moreover, the strategic use of international lawfare and regulatory capture demonstrates the nuanced ways legal mechanisms can be leveraged to advance political or economic objectives. These practices highlight the dynamic nature of legal battles that transcend borders, impacting national policies and governance. To navigate these complexities, nations must continuously strengthen their legal frameworks through transparency, anti-corruption measures, and fostering public trust. Only by addressing these challenges head-on can societies bolster their rule of law and safeguard their sovereignty amidst an ever-evolving global context.

Chapter 7

Infrastructure and Technological Vulnerabilities

Examining the vulnerabilities in critical infrastructure is essential as technology continues to advance and our dependence on it increases. Assessing these weaknesses provides valuable insights into how susceptible our foundational systems are to various threats, both physical and cybernetic. The growing complexity of modern infrastructure, coupled with aging components and insufficient defensive measures, creates a landscape fraught with potential hazards. This chapter delves into these vulnerabilities, revealing the fragility of the systems we rely on daily for energy, transportation, and communication.

In this discussion, we will focus on specific sectors to illustrate the breadth and depth of these vulnerabilities. First, there is an exploration of the energy sector, where outdated power grids pose significant risks. Next, the transportation sector, including logistics, public transport, and shipping infrastructures, will be scrutinized for its inherent weaknesses. Lastly, the chapter evaluates the telecommunication networks and data centers that form the backbone of modern communication, examining their exposure to both physical and cyber threats. Real-world cases are integrated throughout to highlight the profound impact of technological dependence and potential disruptions resulting from cyber attacks.

Analysis of vulnerabilities in critical infrastructure

Examining the vulnerabilities in our critical infrastructure sectors is an essential task as the dependence on technology grows and the risks of cyber threats increase. Understanding these weaknesses helps us take preventive measures to safeguard vital services from various disruptions. This section aims to evaluate the weaknesses in key infrastructure sectors, focusing on energy, transportation, and communications.

Energy: Examination of Power Grid Vulnerabilities and Reliance on Outdated Systems

The energy sector stands as one of the most crucial components of a nation's infrastructure. The power grid, responsible for delivering electricity from producers to consumers, faces several vulnerabilities. One significant weakness is its reliance on outdated systems. Many parts of the power grid infrastructure were built decades ago and have not kept pace with modern technological advancements. This antiquated state makes it susceptible to failures and less resilient to challenges such as cyber attacks or extreme weather conditions (Macaulay, 2019).

For instance, unauthorized access to control systems can disrupt the generation and distribution of electricity. There have been incidents where intruders have gained access to critical data flows necessary for plant operations, posing severe risks to the stability of the power grid. Additionally, the interconnectivity of the US and Canadian energy grids means that a cyber attack affecting electricity supply in one country has the potential to trigger cascading effects in the other (Macaulay, 2019).

Moreover, the energy sector heavily relies on information from the safety sector, which includes law enforcement and first responders. Any disruption in receiving these security reports could impair the sector's ability to prepare and respond to incidents effectively. Furthermore, other sectors often underestimate the importance of timely data from the energy sector, creating a potential threat if this information flow is compromised during critical times. As the frequency and severity of cyber attacks increase, understanding these dependencies and vulnerabilities becomes pivotal in formulating strategies to protect the energy infrastructure.

Transportation: Analysis of Weaknesses in Logistics, Public Transport, and Shipping Infrastructures

The transportation sector is another pillar of critical infrastructure, encompassing logistics, public transport, and shipping infrastructures. Each of these areas is indispensable for the smooth functioning of society and the economy, but they too are riddled with vulnerabilities.

In logistics, weaknesses can be seen in the reliance on complex and interconnected supply chains. A disruption at one node—be it due to natural disasters, cyber attacks, or technical failures—can have a ripple effect on the entire network, causing delays and shortages. For example, the global shipping firm Maersk experienced a major disruption in 2017 when it was hit by the NotPetya malware. This cyber attack brought port operations around the world to a standstill, significantly affecting global trade (Office, 2021).

Public transport systems, including buses, trains, and subways, are vulnerable to both physical and cyber threats. Aging infrastructure, insufficient funding for maintenance, and the increasing reliance on digital systems for ticketing and scheduling create multiple points of failure. In cities where public transport is the backbone of daily commuting, any significant disruption can grind urban life to a halt. The implications extend beyond inconvenience; they affect economic productivity and emergency response capabilities.

Shipping infrastructures also face unique challenges. Ports and shipping lanes are crucial for international trade, but they are exposed to risks from both natural and man-made events. Geopolitical tensions, piracy, and climate change-induced sea-level rise threaten the operational integrity of ports. The 2021 blockage of the Suez Canal by the Ever Given ship underscored the fragility of global shipping routes. It caused an estimated $9.6 billion in trade losses per day, highlighting how a single event can impact the global economy (Office, 2021).

Communications: Evaluation of Risks in Telecommunication Networks and Data Centers

Telecommunication networks and data centers form the backbone of modern communication, supporting both personal and business interactions across the globe. However, this sector is fraught with vulnerabilities that can have far-reaching consequences.

Physical threats to telecommunication infrastructure include natural disasters and intentional sabotage. Hurricanes, earthquakes, and wildfires can damage cell towers and fiber optic cables, leading to widespread communication blackouts. Intentional acts of sabotage, such as cutting undersea cables or attacking data centers, can similarly cripple communication networks. The Department of Homeland Security's Cybersecurity and Infrastructure Security Agency (CISA) has identified these physical threats as serious concerns (Office, 2021).

Cyber-related threats are equally critical. The growing complexity and interdependency of telecommunication networks make them prime targets for cyber attacks. Unauthorized access, malware, and distributed denial-of-service (DDoS) attacks can disrupt services for millions of users. Moreover, telecommunication networks depend on other critical infrastructure sectors—particularly energy, information technology, and transportation systems. Any disruption in these sectors can severely impact telecommunication operations. For instance, a power outage could disable data centers, while a logistic delay might hinder the repair and maintenance of communication hardware (Office, 2021).

Human threats, including insider threats and human error, pose additional risks. Employees with malicious intent or those who inadvertently compromise security protocols can cause significant disruptions. Training and stringent security measures are crucial in mitigating these risks, but they cannot eliminate them entirely.

The private sector owns and operates the majority of the communications infrastructure, making public-private partnerships essential for sector resilience. However, the CISA has not yet assessed the effectiveness of its programs to support the communications sector adequately. This lack of assessment hampers the ability to identify which infrastructure owners and operators benefit most from cybersecurity programs and where improvements are needed. Updating plans and assessing program effectiveness can help set priorities and address emerging threats more effectively (Office, 2021).

Impact of technological dependence and cyber attack vulnerabilities

The rapid digitization of various sectors has led to an increased reliance on digital systems for everyday operations. This technological dependence means that critical infrastructure such as power grids, water supplies, and transportation networks are now heavily integrated with digital technologies. The convenience and efficiency brought about by this digital transformation cannot be overstated. However, it also introduces a myriad of vulnerabilities.

Technological dependence underscores our society's shift towards integrating advanced digital systems into almost every aspect of daily life. From smart cities that manage resources efficiently to businesses using sophisticated software to streamline operations, the reliance on technology is evident. Digital systems facilitate everything from basic communication to complex industrial processes, making them indispensable. Yet, this growing dependence brings with it significant risks.

Cyber attacks have emerged as a prominent threat targeting critical infrastructure. As technology evolves, so do the tactics employed by cybercriminals. With increasing frequency, cyber attacks aim at exploiting the vulnerabilities inherent in digital systems. These attacks can range from ransomware that cripples entire networks to sophisticated breaches that steal sensitive information. Governments and organizations worldwide recognize the gravity of these threats and the potential damage they can inflict.

For instance, cyber attacks on critical infrastructure can lead to severe disruptions. Consider the 2015 Ukraine power grid cyber attack, where hackers managed to disrupt electricity supply, leaving thousands without power. Such incidents highlight the cascading effects of successful cyber attacks. When critical infrastructure is targeted, the consequences extend beyond immediate service disruption. There may be far-reaching impacts on public safety, economic stability, and national security.

The consequences of cyber attacks on critical infrastructure can be catastrophic. One successful breach can trigger a domino effect, leading to widespread outages, financial loss, and compromised data integrity. A disrupted power grid, for example, can halt industrial operations, affect healthcare services, and impede emergency responses. Similarly, an attack on water supply systems could pose serious public health risks.

These scenarios illustrate the necessity of robust security measures to guard against such threats.

Given the escalating threat landscape, mitigation strategies are essential to reduce susceptibility to cyber threats. One effective approach involves investing in comprehensive cybersecurity frameworks. This includes deploying firewalls, encryption technologies, and multi-factor authentication to secure digital systems. Regular updates to security protocols are crucial to counter emerging threats. Furthermore, conducting rigorous risk assessments helps identify potential vulnerabilities before they can be exploited.

Employee training is another vital component of cybersecurity. Human error often plays a significant role in successful cyber attacks. By educating employees about best practices in data security and phishing awareness, organizations can significantly bolster their defenses. Periodic drills and simulations can also prepare staff to respond effectively during actual cyber incidents. Incorporating a culture of security within an organization ensures that every member contributes to safeguarding critical infrastructure.

Additionally, developing and testing disaster recovery plans can minimize downtime and ensure continuity of operations. Backup solutions, whether redundant systems or cloud-based storage, are invaluable in preserving critical data during cyber attacks. Regularly tested recovery strategies enable swift restoration of services, mitigating the impact of disruptions.

A collaborative approach is equally important in addressing cyber threats. Governments, private sector entities, and cybersecurity experts must work together to share intelligence, develop standards, and create resilient infrastructures. Public-private partnerships can enhance information sharing about emerging threats and vulnerabilities, enabling more proactive defenses.

Moreover, legislation and regulatory frameworks play a pivotal role in cybersecurity. Adhering to industry-specific regulations and data protection laws such as GDPR or CCPA ensures that organizations maintain high-security standards. Compliance with these regulations not only protects sensitive information but also mitigates legal repercussions in the event of a data breach.

Society's increasing reliance on digital systems necessitates an ongoing commitment to cybersecurity. Awareness campaigns and continued education about digital literacy are essential for individuals and businesses alike. Understanding the importance of cybersecurity and staying informed about the latest threats equips everyone to make safer decisions in the digital realm.

Case studies of infrastructure attacks

The 2015 Ukraine power grid cyber attack serves as a stark example of how vulnerabilities in critical infrastructure can be exploited. On December 23, 2015, hackers successfully compromised the information systems of three energy distribution companies in Ukraine, leading to widespread power outages that affected roughly 225,000 customers for several hours. This attack was meticulously orchestrated, involving complex malware known as "BlackEnergy." The attackers gained unauthorized access to the control systems months before the actual incident, illustrating their ability to remain undetected while laying the groundwork for a coordinated strike.

Upon infiltrating the control systems, the hackers then executed a series of commands to open circuit breakers, effectively cutting off electricity. They further compounded the outage by launching a telephony denial-of-service attack on the customer call centers, making it nearly impossible for affected residents to report the blackout. What makes this incident particularly concerning is not just the immediate impact but the sophisticated nature of the attack, highlighting the significant vulnerabilities that exist within aging power grid infrastructures. The use of BlackEnergy malware and spear-phishing emails demonstrates the increasing complexity and persistence of modern cyber threats.

Moving from Europe to the United States, the 2021 Colonial Pipeline ransomware attack provided yet another alarming case of technological dependence creating significant infrastructural vulnerability. The Colonial Pipeline, responsible for supplying nearly half of the East Coast's fuel, became the target of a ransomware attack carried out by a group called DarkSide. On May 7, 2021, the attackers managed to breach the pipeline's IT network, encrypting critical data and demanding a ransom payment to restore access. The company responded by taking certain systems offline to contain the threat, which unfortunately led to a temporary shutdown of the pipeline's operations.

This event had immediate and far-reaching consequences. Fuel shortages across multiple states triggered panic buying, long lines at gas stations, and price hikes. The disruption lasted for several days, underscoring the fragility of supply chains dependent on key pieces of infrastructure. Although Colonial Pipeline eventually paid the ransom of about $4.4 million in Bitcoin, the incident sparked extensive discussions around cybersecurity resilience and the essential need for more robust protection measures against ransomware attacks. The Colonial Pipeline case illustrates how cyber threats can exploit technological dependencies, causing chaos in sectors critical to daily life.

An even earlier and highly sophisticated attack that targeted Iran's nuclear facilities serves as a somber reminder of cyber vulnerabilities. In 2010, the Stuxnet worm emerged as the first-known malware specifically designed to disrupt industrial control systems (ICS). Developed jointly by the United States and Israel, Stuxnet targeted Iran's Natanz nuclear enrichment plant. It infiltrated the facility through infected USB drives and proceeded to alter the speed of the centrifuges used to enrich uranium. By doing so, Stuxnet caused physical damage to the equipment while reporting normal operations back to monitoring systems, thereby delaying detection.

Stuxnet stands out not just for its technical prowess but also for its strategic objectives. The worm's ability to inflict physical damage on critical infrastructure from halfway around the world redefined the landscape of cyber warfare. The sheer sophistication of the malware—featuring multiple zero-day exploits and advanced payload delivery mechanisms— demonstrates the potential scale and impact of cyber attacks on national security. The success of Stuxnet highlighted the susceptibility of ICS and prompted nations globally to rethink and reinforce their cybersecurity strategies to protect vital assets.

These real-world cases offer significant lessons in understanding infrastructure vulnerabilities and the dire impact of cyber attacks. The Ukraine power grid attack demonstrated the necessity for enhanced monitoring and rapid response capabilities within energy sectors. It underscored the importance of isolating operational technologies from broader IT networks to prevent unauthorized access. Strengthening authentication protocols and continuously updating defense mechanisms against evolving malware are crucial steps to mitigate similar risks.

Colonial Pipeline's experience highlighted the urgent need to secure supply chain networks. Implementing robust incident response plans, regularly backing up data, and employing advanced encryption methods can fortify defenses against ransomware. Public-private partnerships and government regulations, focused on setting cybersecurity standards, play a pivotal role in safeguarding critical infrastructure. Encouragingly, the U.S. government has since emphasized the significance of cybersecurity through executive orders aimed at enhancing national resilience.

Lastly, the sophistication of the Stuxnet attack underscores the need for international cooperation in cyber defense.

Organizations must invest in intrusion detection systems and anomaly detection frameworks to identify unusual activities early. Sharing threat intelligence across borders and industries can help preemptively counter sophisticated attacks. Regularly conducting cyber drills and penetration testing can expose vulnerabilities, enabling entities to bolster their defenses proactively.

Aftermath and responses to infrastructure attacks

The consequences and reactions following major infrastructure attacks are multifaceted and significant. Understanding these dimensions helps us grasp the immediate and long-term ramifications such incidents have on society, the economy, and public policy.

Immediate Aftermath: Short-Term Impacts on Services and Public Life

When a major infrastructure attack occurs, the immediate aftermath is often characterized by chaos and disruption. Essential services—such as electricity, water supply, transportation, and communication systems—can be severely affected. For instance, a cyber-attack on a power grid can lead to widespread blackouts, leaving millions without electricity. This paralysis of essential services affects hospitals, businesses, and households, creating a ripple effect that exacerbates the initial damage.

In the short term, public life becomes highly disrupted. People may find themselves unable to travel to work or school due to non-operational public transport systems. Emergency response services may struggle to operate effectively, further complicating the crisis. Additionally, panic and confusion can spread quickly among the population, leading to increased anxiety and stress levels. Supermarkets might face shortages due to disruptions in their supply chains, causing issues with food security. Banks and financial institutions also suffer, impacting transactions and access to funds.

Long-Term Consequences: Economic and Operational Ramifications

While the immediate effects of an infrastructure attack are often starkly visible, the long-term consequences can be just as devastating but more insidious. Economically, such attacks can cost billions. Restoring damaged infrastructure requires substantial investment, not just to repair but also to upgrade systems to prevent future attacks. Additionally, businesses affected by the disruption may face prolonged periods of reduced productivity and revenue loss.

Operationally, the recovery process can be slow and complex. Infrastructure systems need comprehensive audits and evaluations to understand the full scale of the damage and vulnerability. Long-term service interruptions may necessitate temporary solutions that are costly and less efficient. Beyond the direct costs, there are often peripheral economic impacts such as job losses and decreased consumer confidence.

Further compounding the issue is the strain on local and national economies. Governments may need to redirect funds from other important areas such as education and healthcare to focus on rebuilding efforts. Over time, this reallocation can affect the broader developmental goals of a nation. Industries dependent on the attacked infrastructure sectors may suffer from prolonged inefficiencies, further dragging down economic growth.

Policy Changes: Adjustments in Regulations and Standards Post-Attacks

Following a major infrastructure attack, one of the critical reactions is the reassessment and modification of existing policies and regulations. Policymakers often undertake thorough reviews of current standards and protocols to identify weaknesses that allowed the attack to occur. This process typically leads to the implementation of stricter regulations designed to bolster the resiliency of critical infrastructure.

For example, after the 9/11 attacks, sweeping changes were made to aviation security regulations worldwide. Similarly, a cyber-attack targeting utilities might prompt new cybersecurity standards for energy providers. These adjustments usually include mandatory risk assessments, incident response plans, and regular security audits.

Governments may also establish or enhance specialized agencies tasked with protecting critical infrastructure. These bodies collaborate across sectors to develop best practices and coordinate responses to potential threats. Legislation could introduce penalties for non-compliance with new security measures, ensuring that all stakeholders prioritize safeguarding essential services.

Additionally, international collaboration often increases post-attacks, as nations recognize the interconnected nature of modern infrastructure. Multilateral agreements and treaties can facilitate the sharing of intelligence and best practices. By fostering global cooperation, countries aim to create a unified front against common threats.

Security Enhancements: Steps Taken to Fortify Infrastructure Against Future Threats

Security enhancements are proactive measures implemented to prevent future attacks and mitigate their potential impacts. Following an infrastructure attack, there is generally a heightened awareness and urgency among governments and organizations to fortify vulnerable systems.

One primary step is the adoption of advanced technologies. Enhanced surveillance systems, intrusion detection software, and automated response mechanisms are integrated into existing infrastructure. Smart grids, for instance, are equipped with sensors that provide real-time data on their operational status, allowing immediate identification and rectification of anomalies.

Another crucial aspect is the improvement of cybersecurity defenses. This includes using encryption, multi-factor authentication, and continuous monitoring to protect digital assets. Regular training programs for staff ensure they are well-prepared to recognize and counteract cyber threats. Organizations often conduct simulated attack drills to test the effectiveness of their security measures and refine them based on the outcomes.

Physical security measures also see significant upgrades. This can involve strengthening perimeter defenses, upgrading access controls, and installing robust physical barriers. For sectors like transportation and energy, redundancies are introduced to ensure that if one part of the system fails, others can continue functioning without major interruptions.

Public-private partnerships play a vital role in enhancing security. Governments often collaborate with private sector experts to leverage their specialized knowledge and innovations. Joint initiatives can range from research and development of cutting-edge security technologies to coordinated response strategies during crises.

This chapter has meticulously examined the vulnerabilities within critical infrastructure sectors and the rising dependence on technology. It has highlighted the significant weaknesses in energy, transportation, and communication systems through real-world examples, emphasizing the susceptibility of these essential services to disruptions from both physical and cyber threats. The analysis underscored how outdated systems, complex supply chains, and aging public transport infrastructures create multiple points of failure, while sophisticated cyber attacks exploit these vulnerabilities to cause substantial disruptions.

Furthermore, the discussion emphasized the broader implications of technological dependence and cyber attack vulnerabilities on society and national security. Real-world case studies demonstrated the catastrophic impacts that such breaches could have, affecting everything from power grids to global shipping lanes. The chapter concluded by reiterating the importance of robust cybersecurity measures and collaboration between public and private sectors to safeguard critical infrastructure. Implementing advanced technologies, improving cybersecurity protocols, and fostering international cooperation are pivotal steps towards building more resilient systems capable of withstanding emerging threats.

Chapter 8

Psychological and Social Manipulation

Psychological and social manipulation profoundly affect the very fabric of society. These techniques, covertly used by various actors, shape public perception and influence behavior in ways that often go unnoticed. Manipulators deploy a range of methods to exploit human psychology, targeting emotions, biases, and cognitive vulnerabilities. The subtle yet pervasive nature of such manipulation tactics can lead entire communities, or even nations, to act against their best interests, highlighting the importance of awareness and critical thinking.

This chapter delves into the nuanced dimensions of psychological and social manipulation, providing an in-depth analysis of various methods employed to exert control and influence. It will examine tactics such as fearmongering, subliminal messaging, and propaganda, elucidating how these strategies bypass rational thought to elicit desired actions. An exploration of the impact of disinformation, particularly in the digital age, will illustrate how rapidly spreading false information exacerbates societal divisions. Further, the chapter will discuss the implications of psychological operations (PsyOps) on both enemies and civilian morale during conflicts. Finally, the discussion will extend to the broader destabilizing effects of manipulating public opinion, underscoring the critical need for digital literacy and robust democratic institutions to safeguard society's integrity.

Psychological Warfare Tactics

Psychological warfare tactics are employed to influence emotions, motives, and objective reasoning in a subtle yet powerful manner. Governments, organizations, and individuals use these tactics to shape public perception and behavior. One of the primary methods of psychological operations is to target emotional responses. By eliciting specific emotions such as fear, anger, or hope, manipulators can drive people to act in ways that align with their goals. This manipulation often bypasses rational thinking, making it a potent tool for control.

Fearmongering is a pervasive tactic used in psychological warfare. By preying on individuals' fears, manipulators can drive specific behaviors and compliance. Fear can be induced through exaggerated threats, sensationalist news, or fabricated dangers. For instance, during political campaigns, candidates may exaggerate security threats to garner support for stringent policies. The constant barrage of fearful messages can create an atmosphere of anxiety, leading people to make irrational decisions based purely on perceived threats rather than facts. It is crucial to recognize fearmongering when it occurs and to respond critically by asking for evidence, fact-checking claims, and seeking multiple perspectives.

Subliminal messaging is another subtle technique used to shape perceptions without the target's conscious awareness. Unlike overt propaganda, subliminal messages are embedded within other content and designed to affect attitudes and beliefs subtly. For example, advertisers may use imperceptible cues in commercials to associate positive feelings with their products. Over time, these hidden messages can influence consumer behavior, making people more likely to purchase certain goods without fully understanding why. Understanding how subliminal messaging works can help individuals become more aware of these influences and make more informed decisions.

Propaganda is a well-known method of psychological manipulation aimed at creating pervasive narratives. It involves the dissemination of biased or misleading information to promote a particular point of view. Propaganda can take many forms, including posters, films, social media campaigns, and news articles. During World War II, propaganda was extensively used to rally public support and demonize the enemy. Posters depicting the enemy as monstrous and dangerous were widespread, instilling fear and hatred among the populace. Such narratives were instrumental in maintaining public morale and support for the war effort. Recognizing propaganda requires critical thinking and an understanding of the techniques used to manipulate public opinion.

To counteract these tactics, it is essential to stay informed and maintain a healthy skepticism. Educating oneself about current events and considering multiple perspectives can help develop a well-rounded understanding of complex issues. Fact-checking sources before accepting information at face value ensures accuracy and reduces the impact of false or misleading claims. Engaging in honest discussions with others fosters critical thinking skills and promotes open-mindedness. By empowering individuals with knowledge and critical analysis skills, we can mitigate the power of psychological warfare tactics and make informed choices based on reliable information.

In today's digital age, the rapid spread of misinformation through social media platforms has amplified the effects of psychological warfare. Social media algorithms often prioritize sensational or emotionally charged content, increasing its visibility and further propagating fear, anger, or divisive narratives. Manipulative actors can exploit these algorithms to amplify specific messages and sway public opinions. Therefore, being aware of the underlying motives behind the content consumed online is crucial. A critical approach towards consuming digital information can reduce susceptibility to manipulation.

Furthermore, psychological warfare tactics extend beyond traditional media to include sophisticated disinformation campaigns and targeted advertisements. Disinformation involves spreading false or misleading information intentionally to confuse or deceive the public. These campaigns often aim to destabilize societies and create division among communities. By polarizing public opinion on contentious issues, disinformation can erode trust in institutions and democratic processes. Targeted advertisements use data analytics to tailor messages to specific demographics, influencing their opinions and behaviors based on their preferences and biases. Understanding these strategies highlights the importance of digital literacy and the ability to critically evaluate information encountered online.

Psychological operations also leverage the bandwagon effect, which capitalizes on the human tendency to conform to the majority. By creating the impression that a particular belief or behavior is widely adopted, manipulators can pressure individuals to follow suit. This technique exploits the desire to fit in and avoid being left out, leading to herd mentality. A real-world example is the rise of social media trends, where the popularity of specific challenges or movements drives mass participation. Recognizing the bandwagon effect helps individuals resist the urge to conform blindly and encourages independent thinking.

Testimonials from influential figures and trusted sources are frequently used to lend credibility to manipulative messages. By associating respected individuals with specific viewpoints or products, propagandists can sway public perception effectively. For instance, during product advertising campaigns, celebrity endorsements can significantly boost product sales by leveraging the trust and admiration people have for the celebrity. In political contexts, endorsements from respected leaders or experts can validate particular policies or ideologies. Analyzing the motivations behind these testimonials and scrutinizing the presented evidence can help individuals stay grounded in facts rather than being swayed by authority figures alone.

Loaded language is another common technique used in psychological warfare. This involves using emotionally charged words and phrases to evoke strong reactions and shape opinions. For example, terms like "freedom" and "patriotism" carry positive connotations and can be used to rally support, while words like "terrorist" or "traitor" can incite fear and anger. These terms often lack specific meaning but are powerful in swaying public sentiment. Recognizing loaded language and focusing on the underlying facts and logic can help individuals navigate through emotional manipulation and form well-informed opinions.

Disinformation and Social Media Manipulation

Disinformation and social media manipulation have become major concerns in modern society. With the widespread use of online platforms, the ability to spread false information quickly has increased dramatically. This subpoint delves into the mechanisms behind these manipulations and their profound impacts on public perception and behavior.

One primary method of disinformation is the dissemination of false information, aimed at confusing or misleading the public. This type of disinformation can range from completely fabricated stories to the distortion of factual events. The rapid spread of fake news on social media platforms makes it easier for individuals to encounter misleading content without realizing its false nature. For instance, during the COVID-19 pandemic, misinformation about self-testing methods proliferated, causing confusion and potential harm to public health efforts. Source 1 stresses that fake news spreads faster than reliable reports due to its sensational nature (Aïmeur et al., 2023).

Another tactic used in social media manipulation is the creation of fake accounts and bots designed to amplify specific messages. These automated accounts can generate a false sense of consensus around particular topics by increasing the number of likes, shares, or retweets. Such actions create an illusion of widespread approval or disapproval, influencing real users' opinions and behaviors. The 2016 U.S. elections highlighted this issue when numerous fake accounts were discovered attempting to shape political discourse. Despite efforts by social media companies to combat these deceptive practices, their prevalence remains a significant challenge.

Algorithmic control over content visibility is another powerful tool for manipulating user beliefs. Social media algorithms often prioritize content based on user engagement, which can inadvertently promote sensational or false information. These algorithms are designed to keep users on the platform longer, prioritizing content that elicits strong reactions. Consequently, posts that provoke fear, anger, or outrage tend to be more visible, regardless of their accuracy. Platforms like Facebook have taken steps to reduce the visibility of low-quality content through initiatives like "ClickGap," yet the effectiveness of such measures is often undermined by internal and external pressures (SOCIAL MEDIA MISINFORMATION SCORECARD - DNC, n.d.).

Targeted ads and misinformation campaigns are also employed to sway political views and influence voter behavior. By utilizing data analytics, malicious actors can design highly specific advertisements that target individuals based on their preferences, fears, and biases. These ads can be particularly effective because they resonate with the targeted audience's pre-existing beliefs, making them more likely to accept the information as true. The 2020 elections saw extensive use of targeted disinformation campaigns aimed at manipulating voter perceptions and decisions. Although social media companies have introduced transparency measures for political ads, the challenge persists as evolving tactics continue to evade detection.

The combined impact of these disinformation and manipulation strategies is profound. They not only mislead individual users but also contribute to a broader atmosphere of distrust and division within society. When people are repeatedly exposed to conflicting and false information, it becomes challenging to discern the truth, eroding trust in traditional media sources and public institutions. Moreover, the emotional and psychological effects of consuming manipulated content can lead to increased polarization and hostility among different groups.

Efforts to combat disinformation and social media manipulation must be multifaceted. While technological solutions like improved algorithms and AI-driven detection systems play a crucial role, they alone are insufficient. Enhancing public awareness and media literacy is equally important. Educating users about the nature of disinformation, how to identify credible sources, and the importance of critical thinking can empower individuals to navigate the complex information landscape more effectively.

Furthermore, collaboration between governments, social media companies, and civil society organizations is essential. Regulatory frameworks that mandate transparency and accountability in digital advertising, coupled with robust enforcement mechanisms, can help curb the spread of disinformation. Social media platforms need to uphold rigorous standards for content moderation, even in the face of political and commercial pressures.

Psychological Operations (PsyOps)

Psychological operations, or PSYOP, are a critical element in modern military strategy, aiming to influence the behavior and perceptions of enemies. The coordination of strategic communication is paramount in these operations. By carefully crafting messages, military forces seek to manipulate enemy behavior, disrupt their decision-making processes, and ultimately gain a tactical advantage. These communications are often multifaceted, involving a variety of media channels such as broadcasts, leaflets, and digital content. The goal is to present information in a way that resonates with the target audience's cultural and psychological context, enhancing its effectiveness.

The use of deception and psychological techniques is another cornerstone of PSYOP. Deception strategies can involve spreading false information to mislead enemy forces about military intentions, capabilities, or movements. For example, during World War II, the Allies famously created a phantom army to divert German attention from the actual D-Day invasion site. This tactic involved fake radio transmissions, inflatable tanks, and even false orders, all designed to convince German forces that the invasion would occur elsewhere. Such psychological manipulations are designed to create confusion, delay enemy responses, and force adversaries into making strategic errors.

Information warfare is another key aspect of psychological operations. This involves using data, misinformation, and cyber tactics to disrupt an opponent's decision-making process. By hacking into communication networks, planting false news, and manipulating social media, military forces can sow discord and mistrust among enemy ranks. For instance, during conflicts in the Middle East, insurgent groups have employed sophisticated online campaigns to demoralize opposing forces and gain support from local populations. These efforts can undermine the enemy's ability to make coherent decisions, leading to strategic blunders and weakened resolve.

The impact of psychological operations extends beyond military targets to civilian morale and public perception. During wartime, the home front's support is crucial for sustained military efforts. By shaping public opinion through targeted messaging, governments can maintain civilian morale, encourage enlistment, and ensure continued backing for military campaigns. Conversely, enemy forces may attempt to erode this support by highlighting casualties, questioning leadership decisions, or promoting anti-war sentiments. Effective PSYOP can counteract these efforts by emphasizing victories, reinforcing nationalistic pride, and discrediting enemy propaganda.

Military deception missions play a significant role in psychological warfare. These missions deliberately mislead enemy forces regarding true operational intentions. Such tactics can range from simple misinformation to elaborate schemes involving dummy equipment and falsified plans. For example, Operation Fortitude during World War II successfully convinced the Germans that the Allied invasion would occur at Pas de Calais rather than Normandy, leading to a significant strategic advantage. By creating plausible but false narratives, military forces can compel adversaries to commit resources and focus efforts on the wrong objectives.

Employment of information warfare is increasingly critical in modern conflicts. Cyber warfare, in particular, has become a vital tool for disrupting enemy operations. Cyber-attacks can disable critical infrastructure, steal sensitive information, and spread disruptive misinformation. For instance, Russian cyber interference in various conflict zones has demonstrated how effective information warfare can be in undermining enemy capabilities. By combining cyber tactics with traditional PSYOP methods, military forces can achieve asymmetric advantages, weakening stronger opponents through non-conventional means.

Coordination of strategic communication also involves understanding and leveraging cultural sensitivities. Messages tailored to the cultural context of the target audience are more likely to resonate and induce desired behaviors. For example, addressing religious leaders' concerns or aligning messages with local customs can significantly enhance the effectiveness of PSYOP initiatives. Cultural intelligence is thus essential for developing impactful communication strategies that align with the psychological and emotional landscapes of diverse audiences.

The use of deception in PSYOP is not limited to large-scale military operations. It also plays a role in smaller, tactical engagements. For example, false radio broadcasts or misleading leaflet drops can confuse enemy units, leading them to expect attacks from different directions or overestimate the strength of opposing forces. These micro-level deceptions can have disproportionate effects, creating opportunities for surprise attacks and reducing the efficacy of enemy defenses. Such techniques highlight the importance of creativity and adaptability in psychological warfare.

Impact on civilian morale is a dual-edged sword in PSYOP. While maintaining high morale among friendly populations is crucial, demoralizing enemy civilians can also be strategically advantageous. Lowered morale can lead to decreased support for the war effort, protests, and even uprisings against enemy leadership. By broadcasting messages that highlight the futility of resistance, the harsh realities of war, or the potential benefits of surrender, PSYOP can undermine the enemy's civilian support base. This, in turn, can pressure enemy governments to reconsider their positions, potentially leading to negotiations or concessions.

Public perception is another critical arena for PSYOP. Modern conflicts are often fought in the court of public opinion as much as on the battlefield. Media coverage, both domestic and international, can shape perceptions of legitimacy, morality, and overall progress. By steering this narrative, military forces can gain broader support and isolate enemies diplomatically. Techniques such as embedding journalists, releasing strategically timed information, and countering enemy propaganda are all part of this effort. The ultimate aim is to create a favorable informational environment that supports military objectives and undermines opposition efforts.

Public Opinion Manipulation and Societal Destabilization

Public opinion manipulation and societal destabilization represent significant threats to the fabric of democratic societies. These tactics often employ sophisticated psychological and social methods that can lead to widespread unrest and long-term damage to societal structures.

Case studies where manipulation led to societal unrest

Examining real-world examples illustrates the profound impact that manipulation can have on public opinion and, consequently, on societal stability. One such case is the Brexit referendum in the United Kingdom. In this instance, various political campaigns utilized targeted misinformation to sway voters. False claims about the financial benefits of leaving the European Union and misleading information about immigration fueled a deeply polarized public debate. The resulting decision to leave the EU has led to ongoing political and economic uncertainties, demonstrating how manipulation can create lasting societal turmoil.

Another notable example is the role of social media in the Arab Spring. Platforms like Facebook and Twitter were initially hailed as tools of liberation, enabling activists to organize and communicate. However, these same platforms also spread misinformation and exaggerated reports, which intensified emotions and actions among the populace. This duality highlights how manipulation through digital means can both inspire and destabilize movements.

Examination of divisive social issues exacerbated by external influence

Divisive social issues are particularly susceptible to manipulation, often exacerbated by external actors aiming to destabilize societies for political or strategic gain. For example, during the 2016 U.S. presidential election, Russian operatives leveraged social media to amplify contentious issues such as racial tensions and immigration (Sanchez & Middlemass, 2022). By creating fake accounts and spreading inflammatory content, they deepened existing societal divides. This external influence not only muddied the waters of public discourse but also sowed distrust in democratic institutions.

Similar tactics have been employed in other contexts, such as the Catalan independence referendum in Spain. External actors spread misleading information to heighten regional tensions, turning what could have been a peaceful political process into a source of considerable unrest. This manipulation underscores the vulnerability of societies already grappling with internal divisions.

Analysis of media's role in shaping and polarizing opinions

The media plays a crucial role in shaping public opinions, and its influence can be a double-edged sword. On one hand, objective journalism provides the public with essential information needed for informed decision-making. On the other hand, biased or sensationalist media can exacerbate divisions and perpetuate misinformation. For instance, cable news networks in the United States often cater to specific political ideologies, presenting news in a way that reinforces viewers' existing beliefs. This phenomenon, known as echo chambers, limits exposure to differing viewpoints and fuels polarization.

Social media platforms further complicate this landscape. Algorithms designed to maximize engagement often prioritize sensational content, leading to the widespread dissemination of misleading or emotionally charged information. The role of bots and fake accounts in amplifying certain messages cannot be overstated. During the COVID-19 pandemic, for example, misinformation about the virus and vaccines spread rapidly on social media, influencing public behaviors and attitudes towards health measures (G, 2022). This manipulation made it more challenging to achieve public consensus on safety protocols, highlighting the media's potent role in shaping societal outcomes.

Long-term consequences on democratic institutions and societal stability

The persistent manipulation of public opinion has dire long-term consequences for democratic institutions and overall societal stability. Eroding trust in these institutions makes it difficult for them to function effectively. When citizens lose faith in electoral processes, judicial systems, or legislative bodies, the legitimacy of these entities comes into question. This erosion of trust can lead to decreased voter turnout, heightened political cynicism, and increased susceptibility to authoritarian tendencies.

In countries like Hungary and Turkey, democratic backsliding has been facilitated by manipulative tactics used by those in power to silence dissent and control public discourse. By undermining free press and weakening the rule of law, these leaders create an environment where misinformation thrives, further destabilizing society (Smith, 2021).

Moreover, the impact of sustained misinformation on social cohesion is profound. Polarization intensifies in-group/out-group dynamics, making compromise and collective action more challenging. For example, in the United States, political polarization has reached levels where bipartisan cooperation is increasingly rare, hindering effective governance. Such division can lead to extremism and violence, threatening the very foundation of democratic societies.

Implications for future stability and recommended interventions

Given the significant threats posed by public opinion manipulation and societal destabilization, proactive measures are essential. Governments must invest in robust cybersecurity frameworks to protect against foreign interference in elections and public discourse. Collaboration between governments, tech companies, and civil society organizations can help develop strategies to counteract misinformation and promote media literacy.

Strengthening democratic institutions is equally vital. Transparency in governance, accountability for misinformation spreaders, and support for independent journalism can build resilience against manipulation efforts. Encouraging critical thinking and fostering environments where diverse viewpoints are respected will also help mitigate the polarizing effects of misinformation.

Bringing It All Together

Throughout this chapter, we have extensively examined various techniques used in psychological and social manipulation. From fearmongering to subliminal messaging, the methods to control public perception are numerous and often intertwined. These tactics exploit emotional responses to bypass rational thinking, significantly impacting individual behaviors and societal norms. By understanding how these manipulative strategies work, individuals can develop critical thinking skills necessary to recognize and resist these influences, thus fostering a more informed and resilient society.

The implications of such manipulations extend beyond individual actions to affect larger societal dynamics. The rise of digital media has amplified the spread of misinformation, making it easier for manipulative actors to sway public opinion and deepen societal divides. Disinformation campaigns, targeted advertisements, and the bandwagon effect all play roles in shaping perceptions and driving collective behavior. Recognizing these strategies is essential for maintaining democratic integrity and social stability. A multifaceted approach involving education, critical analysis, and collaboration across sectors can mitigate the impacts of these manipulative tactics, ensuring a well-informed populace capable of making sound decisions.

Chapter 9

The Erosion of Trust

Trust in institutions and leadership is a foundation upon which societal stability has historically been built. Institutions such as governments, judicial systems, educational entities, and media organizations have long been viewed as dependable frameworks that uphold societal norms and provide consistent guidance. Their ability to foster trust has hinged on their regulatory authority, cultural alignment, ethical standards, and operational efficiency. However, recent trends indicate a significant decline in public confidence toward these once-reliable institutions, raising critical questions about the factors contributing to this erosion of trust and its consequences for society.

In this chapter, we will delve into the various elements that have contributed to the deterioration of trust in institutions and leadership. We will explore specific instances where transparency and accountability were compromised, leading to public disillusionment. Additionally, we will examine how the rise of digital and social media has fundamentally altered information dissemination, making it more challenging for individuals to discern reliable sources from unreliable ones. The impact of leadership failures and scandals on public perception will be scrutinized, shedding light on how ethical lapses contribute to systemic distrust. Finally, we will discuss the broader implications of eroded trust, including its effects on social cohesion, civic engagement, and democratic processes, offering insights into potential pathways for rebuilding confidence in our societal pillars.

Erosion of Trust in Institutions

Institutions have historically played a central role in maintaining societal stability and cohesion. Defined by their ability to provide consistent frameworks within which societies operate, institutions such as governments, legal systems, educational establishments, and media entities have traditionally been viewed as pillars of reliability and trust. Their legitimacy stemmed from the political system's regulatory authority, cultural alignment, adherence to professional ethics, and efficient performance. For instance, the judiciary's commitment to upholding the law has made it a cornerstone of social order, while educational institutions have long been celebrated for fostering knowledge and intellectual growth.

Over the years, however, several factors have contributed to a growing skepticism towards these once esteemed institutions. A significant factor is the perceived decline in institutional transparency and accountability. Instances where institutions have failed to uphold their ethical standards or have engaged in corrupt practices have led to widespread disillusionment. For example, financial scandals within banking systems, such as the 2008 financial crisis, revealed deep-rooted issues of inefficiency and unethical behavior, shaking public confidence (Fifty Years of Declining Confidence & Increasing Polarization in Trust in American Institutions, 2022).

Moreover, the rise of digital and social media has fundamentally altered the landscape of information dissemination. The public now has unprecedented access to news and opinions, which can be both empowering and overwhelming. The constant barrage of information, coupled with the prevalence of misinformation, has muddled the public's ability to discern reliable sources from unreliable ones. This environment has fostered an inherent skepticism towards traditional media outlets, with many Americans viewing news organizations as opaque and influenced by corporate and financial interests (Gottfried et al., 2020).

Institutional transparency is further compromised when leadership fails to act with integrity and openness. When leaders within these institutions are perceived as acting out of self-interest rather than the public good, the erosion of trust accelerates. This lack of accountability is often highlighted in sectors like politics and corporate governance. For instance, political leaders embroiled in scandals or corporations avoiding accountability for environmental damage significantly diminish public faith in these entities.

The repercussions of weakened institutional trust are profound and multifaceted. A society that cannot rely on its institutions struggles with cohesion and collective action. For example, movements such as those advocating to defund the police or questioning the validity of electoral outcomes underscore the depth of institutional distrust. When public confidence in key institutions wanes, it becomes challenging to maintain social order and civic engagement. The divisive responses to COVID-19 measures, like mask mandates and vaccinations, reflect how a lack of trust can lead to fragmented societal responses, potentially endangering public health and safety.

Furthermore, the implications extend to the fabric of democracy itself. Institutions play a vital role in upholding democratic principles through fair processes and equal representation. When trust in these institutions diminishes, so does the effectiveness and perceived legitimacy of democratic governance. Research indicates a troubling trend; nearly half of surveyed individuals expressed reservations about their family members engaging with specific institutions like journalism or religious organizations due to partisan divides (Fifty Years of Declining Confidence & Increasing Polarization in Trust in American Institutions, 2022).

Impact of Leadership Failures

Throughout history, examples of trusted leadership have shown us the potential for building and maintaining public confidence. For instance, during World War II, Winston Churchill's leadership in Britain helped buoy the nation's morale amid dire circumstances. His determination, clear communication, and ethical stance exemplified what effective leadership could do to foster public trust. Similar commendations can be given to Franklin D. Roosevelt in the United States, whose New Deal policies and fireside chats created a tangible connection between the government and its citizens, boosting public confidence when it was desperately needed.

In contrast, contemporary incidents highlighting leadership corruption paint a starkly different picture. Consider the Watergate scandal in the 1970s, which deeply eroded American trust in governmental institutions. More recently, various leaders across different nations have been embroiled in allegations of embezzlement, abuse of power, and manipulation of democratic processes. These incidents not only highlight moral failures but also serve as poignant reminders of the fragility of public trust.

A lack of ethical leadership profoundly erodes public trust. Ethical leadership involves transparency, accountability, and a steadfast commitment to the public good. When these elements are missing, the gap between leaders and the populace widens. Max Weber argued that quality leadership requires a balance of personal conviction and responsibility (Robin, 2020). Leaders who prioritize their agendas over ethical practices often adopt a ruthless "ends justify the means" approach. This myopic vision disrupts the fundamental contract between the governed and those governing, leading to systemic distrust.

The consequences of mistrust in leadership are far-reaching, affecting governance and policy-making. When people lose faith in their leaders, it impacts voter turnout, civic engagement, and overall societal cohesion. For example, the COVID-19 pandemic starkly illustrated how countries with weak leadership suffered significantly compared to those led by competent leaders (Godlee, 2021). The erosion of trust can result in non-compliance with public health directives, reduced economic stability, and widespread disillusionment, further complicating crisis management and policy implementation.

The mutually reinforcing relationship between leadership and institutional strength can't be overstated. Good leadership fosters open, democratic systems, which in turn produce competent leaders (Walker, 2021). Inequality of opportunity within leadership recruitment exacerbates the problem, enabling elite closure and rewarding connections over talent. Such environments offer little prospect for emerging capable leaders, thereby perpetuating a cycle of mediocrity and fostering public skepticism.

Effective leadership during crises can reestablish public trust. During the COVID-19 pandemic, some governments successfully gained trust through proactive responses (Kye & Hwang, 2020). Italy, for instance, witnessed an initial spike in institutional trust due to decisive government actions (Falcone et al., 2020). This underscores the capacity of leadership to restore faith if they govern effectively and fairly.

Moreover, the qualities of presidential leadership directly influence trust in government. Studies show that attributes such as visionary insight, communication skills, effective management, problem-solving abilities, and integrity are crucial for establishing trust (Nam & Lee, 2021). Visionary leaders inspire hope and direction, while good communicators build rapport and transparency with citizens. Efficient management ensures government operations run smoothly, and the ability to solve complex problems showcases competence. Integrity remains paramount, serving as the moral compass for all other qualities.

Historical figures like Nelson Mandela exemplify these traits through their tenure. Mandela's vision for a unified South Africa resonated deeply with his people, earning him immense respect and trust. Similarly, his communication and empathy enabled him to bridge divides and build strong national policies.

On the contrary, examples abound of leaders who failed due to lacking these essential qualities. Corruption scandals involving top executives and heads of state reveal how easily public trust can be shattered. These lapses diminish the perceived legitimacy of the entire governance structure, making it difficult for even well-intentioned policies to gain traction. This deterioration is not merely theoretical; it manifests in lower voter turnout, increased civil unrest, and a general sense of disillusionment among the population.

Consequently, the breakdown in trust has a ripple effect on governance and policy. When the electorate loses faith in its leaders, the democratic process itself is undermined. Disenchanted citizens may turn to extremist ideologies, further polarizing the political landscape. Policies become harder to implement as the government struggles to secure buy-in from a skeptical populace. Essentially, governance becomes reactive rather than proactive, constantly trying to manage crises of confidence rather than addressing underlying issues proactively.

To mitigate these adverse effects, institutions need to focus on cultivating ethical leadership. Recruitment processes must emphasize character, competence, and a commitment to the public good over mere connections and opportunism.

Institutional reforms aimed at increasing transparency and accountability can also restore some degree of public trust.

Scandals and Public Disillusionment

In today's rapidly evolving world, public trust in institutions and leadership is more fragile than ever. One significant factor contributing to this erosion is the impact of high-profile scandals on public perception. Scandals involving corruption or unethical behavior can have a far-reaching effect, shaking the very foundations of trust that citizens hold in their leaders and institutions.

High-profile scandals that shook public confidence include notable incidents like the Watergate scandal in the United States, which led to the resignation of President Richard Nixon. This event left a lasting mark on American politics, instilling a sense of skepticism among citizens toward their government. More recently, the Panama Papers leak revealed widespread tax evasion and financial secrecy by powerful individuals and corporations worldwide, further diminishing public trust in both political and economic systems.

The role of media in amplifying the impact of these scandals cannot be overstated. The advent of 24-hour news cycles and the rise of digital media have ensured that scandals are reported and dissected in real-time. This constant exposure tends to magnify the perceived severity of the issues, leading to a more profound and immediate impact on public opinion. Traditional media outlets often compete for attention, sometimes prioritizing sensationalism over nuanced reporting. Social media platforms add another layer, where information spreads rapidly and can be easily manipulated or misinterpreted, further distorting public perception (Charron & Annoni, 2021).

Frequent exposure to corruption through various media channels has psychological effects on individuals. Studies have indicated that persistent reports of corrupt activities can lead to heightened feelings of distrust and cynicism among the populace. For example, Van Deurzen observed that media reports of corrupt scandals might play an intermediary role between corruption perception and depressive symptoms (Zhang, 2022). This erosion of social trust is closely linked to mental health issues, as continuous exposure to negative news about corruption can exacerbate feelings of helplessness and despair.

The long-term damage to public trust and civic engagement due to frequent scandals is profound. When citizens lose faith in their leaders and institutions, they are less likely to participate in democratic processes such as voting or engaging in community activities. This disengagement can weaken the overall fabric of society, making it more challenging to achieve collective goals and maintain social cohesion. Moreover, a pervasive sense of mistrust can lead to increased support for radical or populist movements, which may exploit these sentiments to gain power, sometimes at the expense of democratic norms.

Restoring public trust after a scandal is an arduous task. It requires not only addressing the specific issue at hand but also implementing broader reforms to ensure transparency and accountability. Institutions must work diligently to rebuild their credibility through consistent and honest communication, ethical behavior, and a commitment to serving the public interest. Leaders need to demonstrate integrity and a willingness to take responsibility for their actions to regain the confidence of their constituents.

Enemies Exploiting Distrust

External forces have skillfully exploited societal distrust, deeply impacting the fabric of our communities. Various adversaries employ a range of strategies to sow this distrust effectively. One common tactic is spreading misinformation—false or misleading information intended to deceive. Misinformation often takes root in environments where people already harbor suspicions about institutions and leadership. For example, adversaries create false narratives that resonate with existing anxieties or societal fractures, amplifying doubts and divisions among different groups.

Propaganda, another potent tool, operates by disseminating biased or misleading information to promote a specific agenda. This method leverages deep-seated emotions and prejudices, making it easier for adversaries to manipulate public opinion. Propaganda can be particularly effective when it plays into cultural symbols, historical grievances, or existing social tensions, creating an 'us versus them' mentality that undermines trust in established institutions.

Social media platforms have become crucial battlegrounds for these activities. Algorithms designed to maximize user engagement often amplify sensationalist content, including misinformation and propaganda. The 'filter bubble' phenomenon exacerbates this issue by isolating users within echo chambers that reinforce their preexisting beliefs while shielding them from diverse perspectives. Consequently, individuals are less likely to encounter contradicting viewpoints, making it easier for misinformation to spread unchallenged (Schleffer & Miller, 2021).

The impact of misinformation and propaganda on trust cannot be overstated. Falsehoods spread rapidly through social networks, often outpacing efforts to debunk them. Studies have shown that misinformation travels faster and reaches more people compared to accurate information. This rapid dissemination fosters a climate of confusion and suspicion, weakening the credibility of legitimate news sources and experts. The erosion of trust extends beyond immediate political contexts, affecting broader societal cohesion and cooperation.

Case studies demonstrate how external forces have successfully exploited societal rifts to weaken trust. A notable example is the 2016 U.S. presidential election, where Russian operatives used social media to disseminate divisive content, galvanizing support for polarizing candidates and spreading doubt about the electoral process's integrity. By targeting vulnerable demographic groups and exploiting existing social divisions, these operatives managed to create significant discord and mistrust, destabilizing democratic processes (Jackson, n.d.).

Another instance occurred during the Brexit referendum in the United Kingdom. Foreign actors were suspected of using social media campaigns to influence public opinion, promoting both pro- and anti-Brexit sentiments with the aim of intensifying divisions. The strategic dissemination of exaggerated or false information contributed to a highly polarized environment, where citizens questioned the credibility of official statements and the legitimacy of democratic outcomes.

Addressing these challenges requires a multifaceted approach. One measure to counteract the spread of misinformation is enhancing digital literacy among the population. Educating individuals on how to identify credible sources, understand fact-checking methods, and critically evaluate information can reduce the susceptibility to falsehoods. Schools and community programs can play pivotal roles in teaching these essential skills, fostering a more discerning and informed public.

Strengthening regulatory frameworks for social media platforms is another critical step. Policies that encourage transparency in algorithmic operations and content moderation can help mitigate the amplification of harmful content. For example, platforms could be required to implement rigorous fact-checking mechanisms and swiftly remove verified false information. Encouraging collaboration between governments, tech companies, and civil society organizations can ensure a balanced approach that respects free speech while combating disinformation.

Additionally, fostering robust independent journalism is vital. Supporting investigative reporting and ensuring journalists have the resources to uncover and verify facts can rebuild trust in the media. Independent media outlets serve as crucial watchdogs, holding power to account and providing the public with reliable information. Public funding models, philanthropic support, and international partnerships can sustain these outlets, safeguarding their independence and integrity.

Community engagement initiatives also offer promising solutions. Initiatives that promote dialogue and understanding across social divides can help bridge gaps and build mutual trust. Local leaders, activists, and community organizations can facilitate these conversations, creating spaces where people can share experiences, challenge misconceptions, and develop a collective sense of purpose.

Lastly, resilience-building is essential. Societies must develop the capacity to resist manipulative tactics and recover from the damage caused by misinformation and propaganda. This involves not only raising awareness about these threats but also nurturing social solidarity and cohesion. Efforts to address underlying issues such as economic inequality, discrimination, and systemic injustice can reduce the vulnerabilities that adversaries seek to exploit.

The chapter has highlighted the gradual decline in public trust towards institutions and leadership, emphasizing the detrimental effects this erosion has on societal stability. Instances of corruption and lack of transparency have led to widespread disillusionment, while the rise of digital media has further complicated the landscape by making it more difficult for people to identify reliable sources of information.

Consequently, a growing skepticism towards traditional pillars such as governments, the legal system, educational entities, and media outlets is becoming increasingly evident. This weakening trust undermines social order and civic engagement, posing significant challenges to maintaining democratic principles and effective governance.

The repercussions of this deteriorating trust are far-reaching, affecting not only individual sectors but the broader fabric of society. As confidence in key institutions wanes, societal cohesion and collective action become more challenging to achieve. The divisive responses to recent events, such as the COVID-19 pandemic, underscore how a lack of trust can lead to fragmented and often polarized actions. Rebuilding this trust requires concerted efforts to enhance transparency, accountability, and ethical leadership. By focusing on these areas, institutions can work towards restoring their credibility and strengthening the essential connection between themselves and the public they serve.

Chapter 10

The Road to Recovery

Recovering from a crisis requires more than just immediate relief; it necessitates a comprehensive and strategic approach tailored to rebuilding and strengthening the nation's core structures. The journey to recovery is a multifaceted endeavor that addresses various aspects crucial for establishing long-term resilience and stability. Understanding how each component—from infrastructure to mental health support—plays a vital role in fostering a nation's capacity to withstand future adversities lays the foundation for effective recovery strategies.

This chapter delves into the essential strategies necessary for national recovery post-crisis. By focusing on enhancing infrastructure, implementing disaster preparedness programs, promoting economic diversification, and bolstering mental health support systems, readers will gain insights into creating a robust framework for resilience. Each strategy is explored in detail, highlighting practical recommendations and examples of successful implementations. This discussion aims to equip policymakers, community leaders, and individuals with the knowledge and tools needed to navigate the complexities of post-crisis recovery and build a stronger, more resilient nation.

Strategies for Resilience

Understanding various strategies to enhance resilience is crucial for national recovery post-crisis. Resilience, defined as the ability of a system or community to resist, absorb, and recover from adverse events, has become an integral part of disaster preparedness and response planning (Sandifer & Walker, 2018). This section explores several strategies aimed at bolstering national resilience by examining infrastructure, disaster preparedness programs, economic diversification, and mental health support systems.

Strengthening Infrastructure to Withstand Future Crises

A fundamental strategy for enhancing resilience involves strengthening infrastructure to endure future crises. Solid infrastructure serves as the backbone of any society, ensuring the smooth operation of daily life and the continued delivery of essential services. In regions prone to natural disasters like hurricanes, earthquakes, or floods, it is vital to build structures that can withstand these extreme conditions. For example, buildings in earthquake-prone areas should be constructed using materials and designs that mitigate shaking and potential collapse. Retrofitting existing buildings to meet updated safety standards can also significantly reduce the risk of catastrophic failure during a disaster.

Investing in resilient infrastructure goes beyond just buildings; it includes roads, bridges, water supply systems, and power grids. Ensuring these critical systems are robust and adaptable can prevent widespread disruption in the event of a crisis. For instance, decentralized energy grids and smart grid technology can help maintain power supply even if one part of the network fails. Similarly, enhancing road networks to allow for quicker evacuation and emergency response can save lives during disasters. Governments should prioritize these investments, recognizing that the upfront costs are outweighed by the long-term benefits of reduced damage and quicker recovery times.

Implementing Comprehensive Disaster Preparedness Programs

In addition to physical infrastructure, comprehensive disaster preparedness programs are essential for enhancing national resilience. Effective disaster preparedness involves creating detailed plans and protocols for responding to various types of emergencies. These plans should be regularly updated and tested through drills and simulations to ensure they remain relevant and effective.

One key aspect of disaster preparedness is early warning systems. Early warning systems provide timely alerts about impending natural disasters, allowing communities to take proactive measures to protect themselves. For example, tsunami warning systems can give coastal residents critical minutes to evacuate to higher ground, while hurricane forecast models can help cities prepare for storms days in advance. The success of such systems depends on their accuracy, the speed of dissemination, and the public's understanding of how to respond to warnings.

Another important component of preparedness is public education and training. Educating the public about how to respond to different types of disasters can save lives and reduce panic during actual events. Schools, workplaces, and community organizations can all play a role in disseminating this information. Additionally, training first responders and equipping them with the necessary tools and techniques ensures they can perform their duties effectively when disasters strike.

Promoting Economic Diversification to Reduce Dependency on a Single Sector

Economic diversification is another critical strategy for enhancing resilience. Nations heavily reliant on a single economic sector, such as oil or tourism, are particularly vulnerable to economic shocks resulting from natural disasters, market fluctuations, or geopolitical tensions. By diversifying their economies, countries can spread risk across multiple sectors, making them more adaptable and less susceptible to catastrophic failure.

For instance, a country that relies heavily on agriculture might invest in developing its technology or manufacturing sectors. This diversification not only provides alternative income streams but also creates job opportunities, stimulates innovation, and attracts foreign investment. Governments can foster economic diversification through policies that encourage entrepreneurship, support small businesses, and invest in education and skill development for their workforce. Public-private partnerships can also play a significant role in helping new industries thrive.

Diversified economies can better absorb shocks and adapt to changing circumstances, ensuring sustainability and social stability. Furthermore, they enable quicker recovery after crises, as the impact on any single sector becomes less debilitating when other sectors can compensate.

Enhancing Mental Health Support Systems to Build Psychological Resilience

Finally, enhancing mental health support systems is crucial for building psychological resilience within communities. Disasters often leave behind more than just physical destruction; the psychological impact on individuals and communities can be profound and long-lasting. Stress, anxiety, depression, and post-traumatic stress disorder (PTSD) are common mental health issues that arise in the aftermath of crises.

To address these challenges, it is essential to have robust mental health support systems in place. Providing accessible mental health services, including counseling and therapy, is a critical step. Communities should have trained professionals who can offer immediate and long-term support to those affected by disasters. Integrating mental health services into primary healthcare ensures that individuals receive holistic care that addresses both their physical and psychological needs.

Public awareness campaigns can also play a role in destigmatizing mental health issues and encouraging people to seek help when needed. Schools and workplaces should incorporate mental health education and support into their programs to foster environments where individuals feel supported and understood.

Rebuilding National Strength

To rebuild and strengthen the nation in the aftermath of a crisis, it is essential to adopt a multifaceted approach that addresses various key areas. Focusing on investments in education and workforce development, supporting small businesses and startups, modernizing healthcare systems, and encouraging innovation and technological advancements can lay a strong foundation for national recovery.

Investing in education and workforce development is crucial for fostering a skilled and adaptable labor force capable of driving economic growth and resilience. One effective strategy involves developing career-connected learning programs that integrate academic education with practical, hands-on experience. The Modern Youth Internship Academy (MYIA) initiative in Northern California serves as an exemplary model by aligning high school curricula with local industry needs through internships, mentoring, leadership projects, college preparation, and career readiness training (*PCRN: Innovation and Modernization Program*, 2018). Such initiatives ensure that students are better equipped with both academic knowledge and practical skills required in today's competitive job market. This holistic approach to education not only enhances employability but also enables young individuals to contribute meaningfully to their communities.

Another vital method for rebuilding the nation centers on supporting small businesses and startups. These enterprises play a significant role in job creation, innovation, and community development. Post-crisis, providing targeted financial assistance, such as grants and low-interest loans, can help these businesses recover and grow. Furthermore, establishing business incubation centers and mentorship programs can offer valuable support and resources to emerging entrepreneurs, thereby nurturing innovation and entrepreneurship at the grassroots level. According to the Pathways to Science: Healthcare, Aquaculture, and Agriculture (PSC) project, creating collaborative regional consortia involving educational institutions and industry partners can facilitate career pathway-aligned dual enrollment opportunities, helping over 17,716 students gain college credits and industry-recognized credentials while still in high school (*PCRN: Innovation and Modernization Program*, 2018).

Modernizing healthcare systems is equally important for achieving better public health outcomes and increasing the overall well-being of the population. Investing in advanced medical technology, expanding access to healthcare services, and improving the efficiency of healthcare delivery are critical components of this process. For instance, leveraging telemedicine and digital health solutions can enhance the accessibility and quality of healthcare, particularly in rural and underserved areas. Additionally, strengthening public health infrastructure by building more hospitals, upgrading equipment, and enhancing emergency response capabilities ensures that the nation is better prepared to handle future health crises.

Encouraging innovation and technological advancements is another key pillar for strengthening the nation. By fostering a culture of innovation, countries can develop new technologies, products, and processes that drive economic growth and improve the quality of life. To achieve this, it is essential to create an enabling environment that supports research and development (R&D) activities, encourages collaboration between academia and industry, and provides funding and incentives for innovative projects. The Regional Work-Based Learning Hub project in Illinois aims to scale equity-driven work-based learning and apprenticeships, ensuring that high school students participate in postsecondary educational and career planning, attain Early College credit, engage in work-based learning opportunities, and earn portable, industry-recognized credentials. This initiative highlights the importance of centralized efforts to address workforce shortages by integrating education and employment systems (<i>PCRN: Innovation and Modernization Program</i>, 2018).

In addition to fostering innovation, investing in digital infrastructure and promoting digital literacy are essential steps towards a technologically advanced society. This includes expanding high-speed internet access to remote and underserved regions, which not only enhances communication but also enables remote work, online education, and telehealth services. Moreover, equipping the workforce with digital skills through targeted training programs ensures that individuals can thrive in an increasingly digital world.

Collaborating with private sector companies and non-profit organizations can also amplify efforts to drive innovation. Public-private partnerships can pool resources, expertise, and networks to tackle complex challenges and deliver impactful solutions. For example, Chemeketa Community College's PSC project creates a consortium involving community colleges, high schools, and industry partners to provide students with dual enrollment opportunities, career planning, and work-based learning experiences in high-demand fields (*PCRN: Innovation and Modernization Program*, 2018). Such collaborations underline the importance of a coordinated approach to education and workforce development.

Continuously engaging with stakeholders, including educators, employers, policymakers, and community leaders, ensures that the strategies adopted are relevant and responsive to the evolving needs of the population. Regular feedback and evaluation mechanisms can help identify areas for improvement and adjust programs accordingly, thereby maximizing their impact.

Finally, fostering a culture of continuous learning and adaptability is crucial for long-term resilience. Encouraging lifelong learning through accessible continuing education programs allows individuals to upgrade their skills and knowledge throughout their careers. This not only enhances employability but also prepares the workforce to navigate changing economic landscapes and technological advancements.

Safeguarding Against Future Threats

Identifying ways to protect against future dangers is pivotal in a national recovery strategy. Ensuring the safety and stability of a nation requires several layered approaches. Among the most critical are enhancing cybersecurity measures, strengthening border security and defense capabilities, diversifying energy sources for sustainability, and establishing robust early warning systems for natural disasters. Each of these aspects provides a foundation upon which a safer, more resilient society can be built.

Cybersecurity has become increasingly important in our digitally interconnected world. As technology advances, so do the threats associated with it. Cyber-attacks can cripple essential infrastructure, compromise sensitive information, and create widespread chaos. Therefore, enhancing cybersecurity measures is not optional; it is an imperative. National efforts should focus on securing networks, protecting data integrity, and developing rapid response strategies for cyber incidents. Investments in advanced encryption technologies, regular security audits, and comprehensive training programs for personnel handling critical data are essential steps forward. Public awareness campaigns highlighting safe online practices can also play a significant role in minimizing risks.

Strengthening border security and defense capabilities is another crucial component. In an era where global mobility is high, and threats can easily transcend borders, robust security measures are necessary to protect national sovereignty. Advanced surveillance systems, enhanced vetting processes, and increased interagency coordination form the bedrock of effective border security. Additionally, investing in cutting-edge defense technologies and maintaining a well-trained military force can act as deterrents against potential aggressors. Coordinating with international allies to share intelligence and best practices also bolsters these efforts, creating a unified front against common threats.

Sustainability in energy consumption is vital for long-term national security. Over-reliance on a single energy source or foreign supplies can expose a country to significant vulnerabilities. Diversifying energy sources—by integrating renewable options such as solar, wind, and hydro power—can mitigate these risks. Governments should incentivize research and development in clean energy technologies and promote policies that encourage energy conservation. Building resilient energy infrastructure capable of withstanding extreme weather events ensures continuous supply even during crises. Furthermore, energy diversification reduces environmental impact, contributing to overall ecological stability and resilience.

Natural disasters present a perennial threat to national security and well-being. Establishing robust early warning systems is a proactive measure to mitigate their impact. These systems leverage technology to detect signs of impending disasters—

such as earthquakes, tsunamis, or severe storms—enabling timely evacuations and preparations. Countries must invest in state-of-the-art monitoring equipment and develop clear communication channels to disseminate warnings promptly. Regular drills and community education programs enhance public responsiveness to alerts, ultimately saving lives and reducing property damage.

The Importance of Unity, Transparency, and Civic Education

In times of national recovery post-crisis, unity, transparency, and civic education become fundamental pillars to rebuild and fortify the nation. Historically, democracies have thrived when these elements are at the forefront of governance and public engagement. Therefore, fostering inclusive political dialogue, ensuring governmental transparency and accountability, promoting civic education, and encouraging community-building initiatives are crucial strategies for a successful recovery.

Fostering inclusive political dialogue and participation involves creating an environment where all citizens feel heard and represented. This means developing platforms and forums that encourage diverse voices and opinions. Inclusive political dialogues help bridge divides across different sectors of society, enabling collaborative problem-solving and policy-making. Involving marginalized communities in political processes can enhance social cohesion and ensure that policies address the needs of all segments of society. For instance, town hall meetings, public consultations, and digital platforms for civic engagement are effective ways to promote inclusive dialogue. These avenues allow citizens to participate in decision-making processes, thereby increasing their investment in societal outcomes.

Ensuring governmental transparency and accountability is another essential component of a resilient recovery process. Transparent governance involves clear communication about government actions, decisions, and spending. This openness builds trust between the government and its citizens, which is particularly important after a crisis when public confidence may be shaken. Accountability mechanisms such as independent audits, public access to information, and robust oversight institutions play a crucial role in maintaining transparency. For example, the establishment of independent anti-corruption bodies can help monitor and report on government activities, ensuring that leaders are held accountable for their actions. Furthermore, regular publication of government expenditures and outcomes can demystify complex governance processes, making them more accessible to the general public. Enhancing transparency not only restores faith in public institutions but also ensures that resources are used effectively and efficiently.

Promoting civic education is vital for engaging citizens in democratic processes. Civic education empowers individuals with knowledge about their rights, responsibilities, and the functioning of government systems. By understanding how their government operates and how they can influence it, citizens are more likely to participate actively in democratic processes. Educational programs in schools, community centers, and online platforms can provide comprehensive curricula covering topics such as voting rights, legal frameworks, and civic duties. Additionally, collaborations with civil society organizations can expand the reach of civic education initiatives, ensuring that even remote or underprivileged communities are included. Engaging youth in particular is essential, as they represent the future electorate and leaders. Programs like mock elections, debate clubs, and volunteer opportunities in community projects can foster a sense of civic responsibility among young people.

Encouraging community-building initiatives to strengthen social cohesion cannot be overlooked in the road to recovery. Social cohesion refers to the bonds that unite members of a society, fostering mutual respect, trust, and solidarity. Community-building initiatives can take various forms, including cultural exchanges, neighborhood improvement projects, and local festivals. Such activities create opportunities for people from different backgrounds to interact, share experiences, and build common goals. For instance, organizing community clean-up drives or beautification projects can bring residents together, fostering a sense of pride and ownership in their local environment. Moreover, community-based organizations and local leaders can play pivotal roles in mediating conflicts and promoting inclusivity. By addressing local concerns and facilitating dialogue among diverse groups, these initiatives contribute to a more harmonious and resilient society.

In this chapter, we have delved into various strategies to enhance national resilience in the face of crises. Strengthening infrastructure ensures that essential services continue during emergencies, while comprehensive disaster preparedness programs enable timely and effective responses. Economic diversification reduces vulnerability by spreading risk across multiple sectors, making nations more adaptable to unforeseen events. Additionally, robust mental health support systems are essential for addressing the psychological aftermath of disasters, promoting recovery, and maintaining community well-being.

These approaches collectively contribute to a robust framework for national recovery. Ensuring resilient infrastructure and preparedness minimizes physical and logistical disruptions, while economic diversification and mental health support address both financial stability and societal cohesion. By implementing these strategies, nations can better withstand future challenges and recover more swiftly and effectively from crises. Each element plays a crucial role in fostering a stable, secure, and resilient society capable of thriving despite adversities.

Conclusion

As we draw this discussion to a close, it's important to reflect on the key threats and vulnerabilities that have been meticulously explored throughout these chapters. Our journey has highlighted a multitude of challenges that confront our nation, ranging from cyber threats to physical infrastructure weaknesses, political divisiveness, and social disparities. Each of these represents a critical point of concern that demands our collective attention and action.

The digital age has ushered in unprecedented conveniences but also unparalleled risks. Cyberattacks have become more sophisticated, targeting not only government institutions but also private businesses and individuals. Data breaches and ransomware attacks highlight our vulnerability to invisible adversaries lurking in the virtual world. Our reliance on technology, while beneficial, exposes us to significant risks that can disrupt daily life and national security.

Similarly, our physical infrastructure is not immune to threats. Aging bridges, roads, energy grids, and water systems pose a continuous risk. Natural disasters, amplified by climate change, further strain these systems, leading to catastrophic failures. These vulnerabilities underscore the urgent need for comprehensive assessments and robust investments to modernize and fortify our infrastructure.

Moreover, the political landscape presents its own set of challenges. The increasing polarization within our political system hampers effective governance and problem-solving. When leaders and citizens are divided along ideological lines, the ability to address pressing national issues is significantly weakened. This disunity detracts from the core principles upon which our nation was founded—unity, liberty, and the pursuit of common good.

Social disparities compound these threats, as economic inequality, racial injustices, and access to education and healthcare remain pressing issues. These inequities not only affect the quality of life for many Americans but also hinder the overall resilience of our society. A nation is strongest when all its citizens have the opportunity to thrive, yet significant portions of our population remain marginalized and underserved.

In light of these numerous threats, it becomes evident that reclaiming America's future requires a concerted effort to enhance our national resilience and unity. It is imperative that we take actionable steps towards strengthening our defenses against these diverse challenges. Collaboration across all sectors—government, private, and civil society—is essential.

To begin with, addressing cyber threats demands heightened cybersecurity measures and public awareness. Investing in advanced technologies, fostering innovation, and implementing stringent security protocols can shield us from malicious actors. Furthermore, public-private partnerships can play a crucial role in defending critical infrastructure from both virtual and physical attacks.

Investments in physical infrastructure must be prioritized. Building resilient structures capable of withstanding natural and man-made disasters is not merely an option but a necessity. Modernizing transportation networks, upgrading energy grids, and ensuring sustainable water management systems will protect our communities and stimulate economic growth.

The reparation of our political fabric is equally critical. Promoting civil discourse and bridging divides through dialogue and mutual respect can restore faith in democratic processes. Encouraging bipartisan collaboration and policy-making based on evidence and pragmatism can lead to solutions that benefit all Americans.

Addressing social disparities calls for comprehensive and inclusive policies that provide equal opportunities for all members of our society. This involves reforms in education, healthcare, and the criminal justice system. By ensuring equitable access to resources and opportunities, we fortify the very foundation of our nation's resilience.

While the path ahead is undoubtedly challenging, it is also filled with promise. Our history is rich with examples of overcoming adversity through innovation, determination, and unity. Just as previous generations confronted and conquered their challenges, so too can we rise to meet ours. The vision of a restored and fortified America lies within our reach, but it requires unwavering commitment and shared purpose.

Imagine an America where our digital networks are secure, providing a safe environment for commerce, communication, and innovation. Picture a landscape where our physical infrastructure is robust and sustainable, capable of withstanding the forces of nature and the passage of time. Envision a society where political differences are navigated through respectful discourse, leading to solutions that propel us forward. Visualize a community where every individual has the opportunity to succeed, free from the burdens of systemic inequality and injustice.

This hopeful vision is not a distant dream but a tangible reality that can be achieved through deliberate action and collective effort. By recognizing our vulnerabilities and actively working to address them, we build a stronger, more resilient nation that can face future challenges with confidence.

In conclusion, reclaiming America's future hinges on our ability to confront and mitigate the myriad of threats we face today. It requires a unified approach, leveraging the strengths and capabilities of every sector of society. Through vigilance, investment, and cooperation, we can transform our vulnerabilities into opportunities for growth and renewal. Let us embrace this call to action with determination and optimism, knowing that a brighter, more secure future for America is within our grasp. Together, we can restore and fortify our nation, ensuring that it remains a beacon of hope, freedom, and opportunity for generations to come.

Epilogue

As we close the pages of this book, it is imperative to pause and reflect on the profound lessons drawn from both historical and contemporary challenges. Each era, each obstacle, and each triumph has etched indelible marks on our collective consciousness, shaping who we are today and guiding us toward a more resilient tomorrow.

History is replete with events that have tested the mettle of nations, forcing them to adapt or perish. From ancient empires to modern states, the trials faced by societies have evolved, but the underlying essence remains constant: the need for vigilance, adaptation, and an unwavering commitment to preserving national identity and values.

Vigilance stands as a cornerstone of any thriving society. The chronicles of history remind us that complacency can lead to downfall. Whether defending against external threats or recognizing internal dissent, a vigilant populace is crucial for safeguarding liberty and sovereignty. Modern times are no different; the threats may have transformed, but their potential impact is as significant as ever. Cybersecurity breaches, economic espionage, and ideological warfare are contemporary manifestations of age-old dangers. By being vigilant, we maintain the ability to preempt and respond to these evolving threats effectively.

Adaptation, the second pillar of resilience, is a testament to human ingenuity and survival. Societies that have adapted to changing circumstances have thrived, while those resistant to change have faded into obscurity. Our journey through time illustrates myriad examples where adaptability has proven essential. The industrial revolution, technological advancements, and shifts in geopolitical landscapes demanded countries to innovate and evolve continuously. Today, the rapid pace of innovation calls for an even greater degree of flexibility. Embracing technological advancements, fostering scientific research, and nurturing creativity are paramount to staying ahead in this relentless race. Adaptation is not merely about survival; it is about seizing opportunities for growth and advancement.

Maintaining national identity and values amidst these changes forms the final pillar of a robust future. Every nation is built on a unique foundation of cultural heritage, traditions, and shared values that bind its people together. These elements provide a sense of belonging and purpose, which is vital for societal cohesion. As we navigate the complexities of globalization, preserving our national identity becomes increasingly challenging yet significantly more critical. The influx of diverse ideas and cultures enriches a nation, but it also poses a risk of diluting core values. Striking a balance between embracing diversity and upholding intrinsic values is essential. This balance ensures that progress does not come at the cost of losing what makes a nation distinct.

In synthesizing these pillars—vigilance, adaptation, and maintaining national identity and values—one can derive actionable wisdom for future endeavors. The lessons gleaned from historical narratives are not mere tales of yesteryear; they are blueprints for forging a resilient path forward. Recognizing patterns, understanding outcomes, and applying these insights to present-day situations is crucial for informed decision-making. Historical reflection equips us with the foresight needed to navigate uncertainties and emerge stronger.

Contemporary challenges, too, offer invaluable lessons. The global response to pandemics, economic crises, and climate change exemplifies humanity's collective strength and solidarity. These challenges transcend borders, necessitating a collaborative approach. By learning from these experiences, we can build frameworks that promote international cooperation and mutual support. This interconnectedness underscores the importance of empathy, compassion, and a shared vision for a better world.

Moreover, the pursuit of innovation should be guided by ethical considerations rooted in our national values. Technological advancements hold immense potential for societal improvement, but they also pose ethical dilemmas. Striking a balance between progress and moral responsibility is imperative. As we anticipate future developments, we must ensure that they align with the principles of justice, equity, and human dignity.

Education emerges as a pivotal factor in fortifying these pillars. An informed and educated citizenry serves as the bedrock of a resilient nation. By instilling the values of critical thinking, adaptability, and civic responsibility in future generations, we equip them to face forthcoming challenges with confidence and competence. Education transcends rote learning; it empowers individuals to question, to innovate, and to contribute meaningfully to society.

In contemplating the legacy we wish to leave behind, it becomes evident that our actions today shape the narrative of tomorrow. History will judge us by how we respond to contemporary challenges and prepare for the future. By fostering a culture of vigilance, embracing adaptation, and upholding our national identity and values, we pave the way for a prosperous and enduring legacy.

This conclusion is not an endpoint but a call to action. It beckons us to take the lessons learned and apply them proactively. Each individual holds the power to effect change, to contribute to a collective mission of building a secure, adaptable, and value-driven society. Together, we can transform challenges into opportunities, ensuring that future generations inherit a world where resilience is ingrained in every fabric of society.

As we turn this final page, let us carry these reflections forward, embedding them into the very essence of our daily lives. Vigilance, adaptation, and the preservation of our national identity and values are not mere ideals—they are imperatives for a future that honors the past while ambitiously striving towards a brighter horizon. The journey continues, and with it, the steadfast resolve to shape a future defined by resilience and unity.

References

Chapter 1

Foreign Influence Operations and Disinformation | Cybersecurity and Infrastructure Security Agency CISA. (n.d.). Www.cisa.gov. https://www.cisa.gov/topics/election-security/foreign-influence-operations-and-disinformation

Kleinfeld, R. (2023, September 5). *Polarization, Democracy, and Political Violence in the United States: What the Research Says.* Carnegie Endowment for International Peace; Carnegie Endowment for International Peace. https://carnegieendowment.org/2023/09/05/polarization-democracy-and-political-violence-in-united-states-what-research-says-pub-90457

Tackling Disinformation, Foreign Information Manipulation & Interference | EEAS Website. (n.d.). Www.eeas.europa.eu. https://www.eeas.europa.eu/eeas/tackling-disinformation-foreign-information-manipulation-interference_en

Understanding and Addressing Social Polarization Between Distinct Groups in America: Can We Bridge The Gap? - Democratic Erosion. (2024, April 11). Www.democratic-Erosion.com. https://www.democratic-erosion.com/2024/04/11/understanding-and-addressing-social-polarization-between-distinct-groups-in-america-can-we-bridge-the-gap/

Chapter 2

Bateman, J. (2022, April 25). *U.S.-China Technological "Decoupling": A Strategy and Policy Framework.* Carnegie Endowment for International

Peace; Carnegie Endowment for International Peace. https://carnegieendowment.org/2022/04/25/u.s.-china-technological-decoupling-strategy-and-policy-framework-pub-86897

Brando, D., Kotidis, A., Kovner, A., Lee, M., & Schreft, S. L. (2022, May 12). *Implications of Cyber Risk for Financial Stability*. Www.federalreserve.gov. https://www.federalreserve.gov/econres/notes/feds-notes/implications-of-cyber-risk-for-financial-stability-20220512.html

China uses coercion, subterfuge and force to spread its influence across the world. (2020, September 1). The Economic Times. https://m.economictimes.com/news/defence/china-uses-coercion-subterfuge-and-force-to-spread-its-influence-across-the-world/articleshow/77866982.cms

Herkenrath, M. (2014, December 19). *Illicit Financial Flows and their Developmental Impacts: An Overview*. International Development Policy | Revue Internationale de Politique de Développement; Institut de hautes études internationales et du développement. http://journals.openedition.org/poldev/1863

International Crime Control Strategy. (2019). Archives.gov. https://clintonwhitehouse4.archives.gov/WH/EOP/NSC/html/documents/iccs-frm.html

Ministry of Foreign Affairs of the People's Republic of China. (2023, February). *US Hegemony and Its Perils*. Www.fmprc.gov.cn. https://www.fmprc.gov.cn/mfa_eng/wjbxw/202302/t20230220_11027664.html

Natalucci, F., Qureshi, M., & Suntheim, F. (2024, April 9). *Rising Cyber Threats Pose Serious Concerns for Financial Stability*. IMF. https://www.imf.org/en/Blogs/Articles/2024/04/09/rising-cyber-threats-pose-serious-concerns-for-financial-stability

- THE RISKS OF FINANCIAL MODELING: VAR AND THE ECONOMIC MELTDOWN. (n.d.). Www.govinfo.gov. Retrieved September 21, 2023, from

https://www.govinfo.gov/content/pkg/CHRG-111hhrg51925/html/CHRG-111hhrg51925.htm

Chapter 3

Alasuutari, P., & Kangas, A. (2020, October). *The global spread of the concept of cultural policy.* Poetics. https://doi.org/10.1016/j.poetic.2020.101445

Davison, W. P. (2020, November 13). *Public opinion - Mass media and social media.* Encyclopedia Britannica. https://www.britannica.com/topic/public-opinion/Mass-media-and-social-media

Disarming Disinformation. (2024, February 8). United States Department of State. https://www.state.gov/disarming-disinformation/

Happer, C., & Philo, G. (2013, December 16). *The Role of the Media in the Construction of Public Belief and Social Change.* Journal of Social and Political Psychology. https://doi.org/10.5964/jspp.v1i1.96

The Impact of Language Ideologies in Schools. (n.d.). ASCD. https://www.ascd.org/el/articles/the-impact-of-language-ideologies-in-schools

Understanding Ideology in Educational Contexts • Teachers Institute. (2023, December 18). https://teachers.institute/societal-context-of-education/understanding-ideology-education/

Ulloa, R., Kacperski, C., & Sancho, F. (2016, April 8). *Institutions and Cultural Diversity: Effects of Democratic and Propaganda Processes on Local Convergence and Global Diversity* (B. Podobnik, Ed.). PLOS ONE. https://doi.org/10.1371/journal.pone.0153334

West, D. M. (2017, December 18). *How to combat fake news and disinformation.* Brookings; The Brookings Institution. https://www.brookings.edu/articles/how-to-combat-fake-news-and-disinformation/

Chapter 4

Arnaudo, D., Bradshaw, S., Ooi, H. H., Schwalbe, K., Studdart, A., Zakem, V., & Zink, A. (2021, September 28). *Combating Information Manipulation: A Playbook for Elections and Beyond*. International Republican Institute. https://www.iri.org/resources/combating-information-manipulation-a-playbook-for-elections-and-beyond/

Election Misinformation | Brennan Center for Justice. (n.d.). Www.brennancenter.org. https://www.brennancenter.org/election-misinformation

Lobbying and Political Activities | Emory University | Atlanta GA. (n.d.). Staging.web.emory.edu. https://finance.emory.edu/home/financedivision/accounting/tax/lobbying-political-activities.html

Perkins, C. (2020, September 23). *A History of Corruption in the United States*. Harvard Law School; The President and Fellows of Harvard College. https://hls.harvard.edu/today/a-history-of-corruption-in-the-united-states/

Russian Cyber Actors are Exploiting a Known Vulnerability with Worldwide Impact. (n.d.). National Security Agency/Central Security Service. https://www.nsa.gov/Press-Room/Press-Releases-Statements/Press-Release-View/Article/3616384/russian-cyber-actors-are-exploiting-a-known-vulnerability-with-worldwide-impact/

The Era of Manipulation. (n.d.). Journal of Democracy. https://www.journalofdemocracy.org/articles/the-era-of-manipulation/

US department of state. (2022, April 1). *United States Strategy to Prevent Conflict and Promote Stability*. United States Department of State. https://www.state.gov/united-states-strategy-to-prevent-conflict-and-promote-stability/

Weiser, D. (2021, July 12). *Why Lobbying Is Legal and Important in the U.S.* Investopedia. https://www.investopedia.com/articles/investing/043015/why-lobbying-legal-and-important-us.asp

Wei, S.-J. (2001, April 30). *Corruption and Globalization*. Brookings. https://www.brookings.edu/articles/corruption-and-globalization/

Zadrozny, B. (2024, January 18). *Disinformation poses an unprecedented threat in 2024 — and the U.S. is less ready than ever*. NBC News. https://www.nbcnews.com/tech/misinformation/disinformation-unprecedented-threat-2024-election-rcna134290

Chapter 5

Department of Homeland Security. (2013, October 25). *Cybersecurity Insider Threat*. Department of Homeland Security. https://www.dhs.gov/science-and-technology/cybersecurity-insider-threat

Economic Espionage. (n.d.). Www.dni.gov. https://www.dni.gov/index.php/ncsc-what-we-do/ncsc-threat-assessments-mission/ncsc-economic-espionage

Greenwald, G., MacAskill, E., & Poitras, L. (2013, June 11). *Edward Snowden: the whistleblower behind the NSA surveillance revelations*. The Guardian; The Guardian. https://www.theguardian.com/world/2013/jun/09/edward-snowden-nsa-whistleblower-surveillance

Geiger, A. W. (2018, June 4). *How Americans have viewed government surveillance and privacy since Snowden leaks*. Pew Research Center; Pew Research Center. https://www.pewresearch.org/short-reads/2018/06/04/how-americans-have-viewed-government-surveillance-and-privacy-since-snowden-leaks/

Nation-State Cyber Espionage and its Impacts. (2013). Wustl.edu. https://www.cse.wustl.edu/~jain/cse571-14/ftp/cyber_espionage/

Objective 2.4: Enhance Cybersecurity and Fight Cybercrime. (2022, March 16). Www.justice.gov. https://www.justice.gov/doj/doj-strategic-plan/objective-24-enhance-cybersecurity-and-fight-cybercrime

Alter, K. J., & Helfer, L. R. (2017, June 22). *Nature or Nurture? Judicial Lawmaking in the European Court of Justice and the Andean Tribunal of Justice*. Oxford University Press EBooks; Oxford University Press. https://doi.org/10.1093/acprof:oso/9780199680788.003.0008

Department of Justice | Strategic Goal 1: Uphold the Rule of Law | United States Department of Justice. (2022, March 16). Www.justice.gov. https://www.justice.gov/doj/doj-strategic-plan/strategic-goal-1

Preston, S. (2015, April 10). *The Legal Framework for the United States*. U.S. Department of Defense. https://www.defense.gov/News/Speeches/Speech/Article/606662/the-legal-framework-for-the-united-states-use-of-military-force-since-911/

Rule of Law | Democracy, Human Rights and Governance. (2022, December 9). U.S. Agency for International Development. https://www.usaid.gov/democracy/rule-law

Tsang, S. (2024, April 4). *Sanctions in Current Geopolitical Climate: Challenges to International Arbitration in the Context of the Russia-Ukraine War*. Kluwer Arbitration Blog. https://arbitrationblog.kluwerarbitration.com/2024/04/04/sanctions-in-current-geopolitical-climate-challenges-to-international-arbitration-in-the-context-of-the-russia-ukraine-war/

The global assault on rule of law. (n.d.). Www.ibanet.org. https://www.ibanet.org/The-global-assault-on-rule-of-law

United States International Cyberspace & Digital Policy Strategy. (n.d.). United States Department of State. https://www.state.gov/united-states-international-cyberspace-and-digital-policy-strategy/

United Nations. (2015). *What is the Rule of Law?* United Nations and the Rule of Law. https://www.un.org/ruleoflaw/what-is-the-rule-of-law/

Chapter 7

Blogger, G. (2024, January 18). *Security in the New World: How Interconnectedness is Raising Security Concerns*. Mead & Hunt. https://meadhunt.com/new-world-security-concerns/

Macaulay, T. (2019, May 9). *The Danger of Critical Infrastructure Interdependency*. Centre for International Governance Innovation. https://www.cigionline.org/articles/danger-critical-infrastructure-interdependency/

Office, U. S. G. A. (2021, November 23). *Critical Infrastructure Protection: CISA Should Assess the Effectiveness of its Actions to Support the Communications Sector*. Www.gao.gov. https://www.gao.gov/products/gao-22-104462

strong, travis. (2023, August 17). *Technology Poses a Threat to your Business | Rea & Associates*. Rea CPA | Just Another WordPress Site. https://www.reacpa.com/insight/navigating-the-risks-how-technology-poses-threats-to-your-business/

Chapter 8

8th POG(A) Home. (n.d.). Www.soc.mil. Retrieved July 25, 2024, from https://www.soc.mil/8thMISG/8thPOGhome.html

Aïmeur, E., Amri, S., & Brassard, G. (2023, February 9). *Fake news, disinformation and misinformation in social media: a review*. Social Network Analysis and Mining. https://doi.org/10.1007/s13278-023-01028-5

G, C. (2022, July 7). *Social Media Misinformation and the Prevention of Political Instability and Mass Atrocities • Stimson Center*. Stimson Center. https://go.nd.edu/334798

G, V. (2023, August 1). *What is Propaganda: Understanding its Definition, Techniques, and Examples.* NetReputation. https://www.netreputation.com/understanding-propaganda/

G, V. (2023, August 8). *The Power and Impact of Propaganda.* NetReputation. https://www.netreputation.com/the-power-and-impact-of-propaganda/

Psychological Operations. (n.d.). Goarmy.com. https://www.goarmy.com/careers-and-jobs/specialty-careers/special-ops/psychological-operations

Sanchez, G., & Middlemass, K. (2022, July 26). *Misinformation is eroding the public's confidence in democracy.* Brookings. https://www.brookings.edu/articles/misinformation-is-eroding-the-publics-confidence-in-democracy/

SOCIAL MEDIA MISINFORMATION SCORECARD - DNC. (n.d.). Democrats. https://democrats.org/who-we-are/what-we-do/disinfo/social-media-misinformation-scorecard/

Chapter 9

Anheier, H. K., & Knudsen, E. L. (2022, December 13). *The 21st century trust and leadership problem: Quoi faire?* Global Policy. https://doi.org/10.1111/1758-5899.13162

Charron, N., & Annoni, P. (2021, February 15). *What is the Influence of News Media on People's Perception of Corruption? Parametric and Non-Parametric Approaches.* Social Indicators Research. https://doi.org/10.1007/s11205-020-02527-0

Fifty Years of Declining Confidence & Increasing Polarization in Trust in American Institutions. (2022, November 15). American Academy of Arts & Sciences. https://www.amacad.org/publication/fifty-years-declining-confidence-increasing-polarization-trust-american-institutions

Gottfried, J., Walker, M., & Mitchell, A. (2020, August 31). *Americans See Skepticism of News Media as Healthy, Say Public Trust in the*

Institution Can Improve. Pew Research Center's Journalism Project. https://www.pewresearch.org/journalism/2020/08/31/americans-see-skepticism-of-news-media-as-healthy-say-public-trust-in-the-institution-can-improve/

Jackson, J. B., Dean. (n.d.). *Countering Disinformation Effectively: An Evidence-Based Policy Guide*. Carnegie Endowment for International Peace. https://carnegieendowment.org/2024/01/31/countering-disinformation-effectively-evidence-based-policy-guide-pub-91476

Nam, K., & Lee, S.-Y. (2021, September 30). *Presidential Leadership Qualities and Their Influence on Trust in Government*. Journal of Policy Studies. https://jps.scholasticahq.com/article/29049-presidential-leadership-qualities-and-their-influence-on-trust-in-government

Schleffer, G., & Miller, B. (2021). *The Political Effects of Social Media Platforms on Different Regime Types*. Texas National Security Review. https://tnsr.org/2021/07/the-political-effects-of-social-media-platforms-on-different-regime-types/

Zhang, Y. (2022, August). *The Relationship Between Corruption Perception and Depression: A Multiple Mediation Model*. Psychology Research and Behavior Management. https://doi.org/10.2147/prbm.s370045

Chapter 10

4 Actions to Help Disadvantaged Communities. (n.d.). ICF. https://www.icf.com/insights/disaster-management/equity-in-resilience

How US employers and educators can build a more nimble education system with multiple paths to success. (n.d.). Brookings. https://www.brookings.edu/articles/how-us-employers-and-educators-can-build-a-more-nimble-education-system-with-multiple-paths-to-success/

Nusir, M., Bell, D. (2017). *Co-design for Government Service Stakeholders*. *Hawaii International Conference on System Sciences*. https://doi.org/10.24251/HICSS.2017.307

PCRN: Innovation and Modernization Program. (2018). Ed.gov. https://cte.ed.gov/grants/innovation-and-modernization-grant-program

Sandifer, P. A., & Walker, A. H. (2018, December 21). *Enhancing Disaster Resilience by Reducing Stress-Associated Health Impacts*. Frontiers in Public Health. https://doi.org/10.3389/fpubh.2018.00373

The State of Democracy in the United States. (2021, December 5). Www.fmprc.gov.cn. https://www.fmprc.gov.cn/mfa_eng/zxxx_662805/202112/t20211205_104 62535.html